Dr. Daniel

M000036008

Destiny: The Other Side of Through

An Anthology

Amazon 2019

ISBN: 978-1-7342003-0-0

Published by Danmil Publishing

. 12650 W. 64th Avenue

Arvada, CO 80004

www.danmilgroup.com

Printed in the United States of America

Table of Contents

Dedication

Destiny: The Other Side of Through is dedicated to the 97 percent of us on the planet, who are still wandering generalities and not yet destiny specific. To the three percenters who are already awakened to your purpose and destiny, we have a dedication request. Please pass a copy of this book to someone else who needs to be awakened just like you.

Acknowledgement

To my wife Millicent and our six children, Daniel Jr., Imani, Michael, Danae, Destiny and James, I am most grateful you have always been my destiny and vision partners. Thank you for surrounding me and allowing me to take the risk of faith to be, do and have all that God has destined for us. Also, thank you for your love and for making personal sacrifices to be there for me and available to God.

Thank you to Dr. Katrina Ferguson and Fig Publications, who midwifed Danmil Publications through this first anthology project. And thanks to all the authors of *Women of Worth*, who allowed me to serve as their project chaplain.

To Ella Coleman and Ellavation Publishing, who wore multiple hats for this project, which include publishing consultant, technical editor, and serving as the writing coach for our first-time writers. You made the words and messages of this book sing with a harmonious sound, so readers understand what God is saying through our messengers, teachings and stories.

To my fellow authors of *Destiny: The Other Side of Through*, you are the synergistic technicians whom the Holy Spirit selected to craft this noble collection of epistles. Thank you for your work, messages, and destiny models that will activate many, who were formerly passive to their destinies, to join the few who change the world. Heaven's economy is going to reward you for the time, talent and treasure it cost you to participate in this kingdom enterprise.

I also want to thank you, valued reader and supporter, for purchasing this book. We look forward to hearing amazing stories as you share with us, how your life shifted vertically and horizontally by the impact of our authors' stories shared in this work.

In case we may have left out the names of some who contributed along the way, please know that we appreciate you very much.

www.osot.life

Email: info@osot.life

Facebook: @osot

Preface

Destiny: The Other Side of Through begins with recognizing that we each have a destiny; more importantly, a divine or God-given destiny. Destiny speaks to that place called *there*--a place in front of us, a future we are in route to. It is s place that, from here, we can only see with the intelligence of God.

A destiny given to us by God means He is personally invested in the fulfillment of our future. God's design for the fulfillment of purpose and destiny is done in a manner that requires Him to take the journey with us. In Eden, where things are done according to God's purpose, God comes to walk with Adam. During the period after Eden but before the flood, God comes to walk with Noah and Enoch. During the period of the Patriarchs, God walks with Abraham, Isaac, and Jacob. And during this time, God comes to walk with you and me.

Destiny is a divine appointment wrapped up within our purpose. Purpose and destiny are created to be unique and specific to an individual. They are personally given to us by God, and a personal, covenant relationship with God is required to arrive at God's expected end for us as individuals. Even though our purpose and destiny are unique to us as individuals, they are designed to intertwine and overlap with the purpose and destiny of other persons.

One thing we understand about the fulfillment of purpose as an individual is that purpose is a picture of the end. Our purpose is that one thing we were specifically created to do. During the journey to our expected end, God, our Covenant Partner provides us with five things:

1. Help

2. Deliverance

3. Acts - of salvation

4. Victory

5. Good Success

The story of the life of Joseph is one of my favorite biographies of a leader. In Joseph's journey to the other side of through, he dreamed a dream and encountered what appears to be a serious reroute. Dreamed and dream in Hebrew are similar words with very different meanings. Châlam is the Hebrew word translated into our English word *dreamed* and has several implications, one of which is "to bind firmly." In other words, God gives Joseph a divine destiny, and then a reroute from being the favorite son occurred. He found himself in the pit, in Potiphar's house, and the prison. During what seemed like reroutes, Joseph's dream was bound firmly to him. When he finally arrived at Pharaoh's house, his dream made all of the reroutes with him. Make sure you hold on to your dream through all of your seemingly reroutes.

Like Joseph, we will have tests and trials while journeying to the other side of through. God, in His infinite wisdom, pre-determined the above five things would be necessary to ensure both success and fulfillment. History teaches us that being tested is less of an issue than how we face the test. To endure until fulfillment is achieved requires us to develop resiliency. In remaining resilient, you must exert yourself and stay active for long periods of time. You must continually refocus to remain focused on your purpose and destiny. Also, you must establish a mindset that gives you the ability to resist, withstand, recover from, and develop immunity to anything that takes you off the journey and has the appearance of failure, until you arrive at the other side of through.

As this anthology unfolds, you will see one example after the other, from the youngest of us to the most senior of us, how God consistently provides these five resources. You will see how God's supply of wisdom is unique and specific to your purpose; how He customizes the strategy to the person, place, and time. So, as you read, observe how going through the process, including the victory of each leg of the journey, manifests His glory.

What you hold in your hand are our stories. However, they are incomplete because we are still walking out our journey with God. Walking with God ensures we arrive at our intended destination, that expected end. While we have not arrived yet, we know there is someplace specific to go — the journey to the other side of through.

Calvin Brown

Top Five Talents: Relator, Learner, Responsibility, Analytical & Strategic

Calvin Brown is the founder and senior consultant at TechnicallyInclined.com. To reach this author for speaking engagements, programs and services email him at calvin@technicallyinclined.com.

To learn more about the author and upcoming OSOT itinerary go to osot.life.

Top Five Talents: Command, Futuristic, Ideation, Input & Deliberative

Chapter 1

What God has made crooked let no man make straight: You are S.H.A.P.E.D. for destiny

"What God has made crooked, let no man make straight." - Ecclesiastes 7:13

By Dr. Daniel Haupt

One thing we all have in common is our entrance into the world with a purpose and destiny. This is a direct route but never a straight line (Jerimiah 1:5). We are all inventions of God's eternal plans, specifically "SHAPED" for a determined destiny, which we must not only discover for ourselves but maximize the potential to fulfill it in our lifetime. We should intentionally aim to reach that place called destiny that is located on *the other side of through*—the place of process and preparation to fulfill greater purpose in one's life. The late Dr. Myles Munroe once said, "The greatest tragedy in life is not death, but life without a reason."

One of the tools to help us pinpoint our purpose or reason for being, is called S.H.A.P.E.D. This acronym is comprised of innate and influenced characteristic criteria for assessing purpose and destiny. It is enlightening to learn and know how you are **S.H.A.P.E.D**: **S** (Special endowment), **H** (Heartbeat), **A** (Ability), **P** (Personality), **E** (Environment or Experiences), **D** (Destiny). Your SHAPE is unique for a special purpose and destiny to impact and profit the generation for which you were born and called to transform. With so many people being clueless of their purpose, why God created them, and put them here, help is seriously needed for clarity and answers.

It is dangerous to be alive and not know the reason why you were shaped with the exceptional charisma that defines your life" (1 Corinthians 9:26). We were not created to wander through this earthly experience aimlessly. We were *shaped* for destiny. There is a destiny preordained for you and me to manifest as citizens of God's Kingdom. God's intention for us is illustrated in how He has shaped us for purpose and destiny. Our *shape* for destiny is our fate to prophetically manifest by purpose and through collaboration to impact the Seven Mountains of Influence in our culture—Family, Health, Education, Religion, Media, Government, and Entertainment. We are all impacted by these and can achieve influence within them when we know God, our purpose, and how to maximize our potential.

Our callings, purposes, and destiny are calculated in the heart of God. Before you were formed in your mother's womb, He already had a plan for you (Jeremiah 1:5). The Maker of the universe is the God of purpose. No matter how many dark days you've seen, God has a magnificent plan for you. You might have fallen seven times seven so hard in the past, but you are still His perfect designed original for *your* destiny. Our destinies on earth are developed in heaven before we take any shape or form as humans. According to scientific studies and Biblical precepts, there were 14 million sperms competing to be *you* at conception, but you were the one God chose to be born the winner. Only one out of 14 million spermicides reached your mother's fallopian tube; a pearliest journey to fertilize the egg, but you were the one who did. In other words, you are not a cosmic accident. Consider the words of God in Romans 8:30. *"For those He predestined,*

He also called, those He called, He also justified; those He justified, He also glorified" (NIV). Notice, according to that scripture, that the foremost thing God does in the process of creating us is to first determine our destinies. God had a plan for us before He called us into being and He preordained a future for us before we are born. It's been said, "Purpose produces design, and design predicts potential." God first had a purpose for you, and then He created and SHAPED your unique design, which always is a prophetic illustration of what purpose and destiny He has in mind for you and me.

However, if you, from time to time, feel like you have not truly found your purpose or recognized how you have been SHAPED for destiny, you are not alone. Most people have a God size void and emptiness in their hearts when they contemplate the many components behind their destiny. Ninety-seven percent of people are wandering generalities and not destiny specific. Like chaff driven by every wave, they live life the way it comes without any real intent or set destiny in mind. Only 3 percent of the population live life on purpose, and that is why only these few ever find true meaning and satisfaction in life. Dr. Myles Munroe said, "Until purpose is discovered, existence has no meaning, for purpose is the source of fulfillment."

Proverbs 20:5 (RSV) explains that *"the purpose of a man is like deep water, but a man of understanding will draw it out."* Life is too precious of a miracle to be squandered. It is a gift to be cherished, and a priceless treasure never meant to be wasted. Its purpose must be discovered, nourished, sustained, and fulfilled. For when our days here are expired, and our toils on earth are over, we will look back over the years, either smiling for a life well lived or regretting for a lifetime that was wasted. We won't have another chance to live again in this time and space, so we should live well and finish strong. No need to wait; start now and start deliberately living a life of purpose. The word of God is simple in Jeremiah 29:11 (KJV): "I know the thoughts that I think toward you, says the LORD, thoughts of peace, not of evil, to give you an expected end."

*"You are a chosen generation, a royal priesthood, a
holy nation, and His own special people, that you may
proclaim the praises of Him who called you out of
darkness into His marvelous light"* (1 Peter 2:9 NKJV).

Earlier, I talked about the Seven Mountains of Influence,
however, world system seems to dominate them much more than
God's chosen people. But God made us to absolutely impact the
Seven Mountains in our culture and generation. The Seven
Mountains of Influence are spheres of dominion and platforms of
impact and authority upon which our true meanings and destinies
are discovered and applied. These are the seven mountains of
Family and Human Development, Priesthood (Religion),
Government, Education, Communication, Entertainment,
Economics, and Entrepreneurship. The way you are made by God
(Elohim) and how you are *shaped* is a prophetic illustration of
how He intends to manifest each of us for our royal priesthood
assignments as kingdom citizens on earth. Your destiny SHAPE
is how you uniquely fit into your space and position on these
mountains. Your destiny SHAPE is why, no matter what your
circumstance is, if you move in faith and obey God, nothing can
stop your destiny and purpose from manifesting and taking you to
the *other side of through*. You are Seven Mountains kingdom
citizen, SHAPED for your destiny.

What does it mean to be S.H.A.P.E.D.?

*"Consider the work of God; for who can make straight
what He has made crooked?"* - Ecclesiastes 7:13 NKJV

To further explain, **S.H.A.P.E.D** is an acronym that explains the
illustrated charisma of God in each person for his/her purpose
and destiny. It determines the creative process of how we are
made and prepared for a predetermined future. It explains the
factors that constitute our beings and that are relevant to our
destinies. A purpose-driven man is always compelled to act
naturally with these dimensions in order to realize his dreams and
calling in life. For example, you might not be fitted into certain
areas or skilled in some things that come naturally to other

people. This does not mean you are less relevant, instead, you are made differently for a different purpose. While in the lens of the world, it might appear as if you are crooked and do not fit for a particular divine intention. The way you are shaped is just perfect for the unique purpose and destiny God has in mind for you. Dr. Myles Munroe made another wise point when he said, "God **shaped** us in an innovative way; He creatively designed us to do His business in our sphere."

God instructed the prophet to go down to the potter's house, where he saw him (the potter) making a vessel of clay. As he stood observing the potter doing his work, the voice of God came to him saying: *"look, as the clay is in the potter's hand, so are you in my hand, O house of Israel"* (Jeremiah 18:6 NKJV). What God is simply saying here is that none of us is a product of a mistake. We are all SHAPED according to His perfect purpose and plan. God seized the moment or your mother and father's connection to make you fearfully and wonderfully with His design. You are deliberately fashioned the way you are for a reason.

Do not forget that the purpose of a vessel determines the way it is made by the potter. For instance, out of the same clay, the potter can decide to make a cup, a pot, a water jar, and a flower vase. These four vessels are made from the same material (clay) by the same potter but with different intentions to serve different motives. While the flower vase might be embroidered with careful artistry, creative designs, and beautiful paintings, the pot, on the other hand, will be made rougher, stronger (to withstand the fire), and less attractive. Each vessel is designed specifically for the purpose it was made.

Isaiah 64:8 (NKJV) says, *"O LORD, you are our Father; we are the clay, and you our Potter; and we all are the work of your hands."* You don't have to be anybody else. You are perfect the way you are. Instead of wishing to become someone else, Psalm 139:14 should be your confession: *"I am fearfully and wonderfully made; your works are wonderful."*

Your strength, abilities, talents, gifts, shortcomings, and flaws are all parts of what makes who you are and who you are meant to be. The purpose for which you are created determines the way you are made, the place you are placed, and the resources you are given. There are no two people with the exact same fingerprints. You should never aspire to live another person's life because you have been specifically SHAPED to be who you are for God's master plan for His earth and eternal intentions when our earthly assignments are over.

Consider the wise words of King Solomon in Ecclesiastes 7:13 (NLT); *"Accept the way God does things, for who can make straight what He has made crooked?"* The way you are S.H.A.P.E.D. is unique and perfect, uniquely designed for your destiny. The potter made the flower vase and the water jar from the same clay but for different purposes. It will be so absurd to see the flower vase serving the function of a clay pot, or the water jar used as a drinking cup. Trying to become what you are not S.H.A.P.E.D for is like trying to make straight what God has made crooked. God is consistent in His plan and design for our lives. He has equipped us to respond to our time and seasons and S.H.A.P.E.D. us with inborn capacities, yearnings, passions, skills, ability to learn, temperaments, and experiences that point us to our purpose and destiny. S.H.A.P.E.D. is an acronym filled with revelation as you will discover below.

S (Special Endowment)

The **S** stands for our array of Special Endowments and gifts God has invested in us. These inbuilt abilities can perform perfectly to solve problems and add value to the lives of those we are called to effect. God has deposited in us His Spirit, which inspires us to greatness (Job 32:8). Speaking of our Special Endowments, Apostle Paul said, *"do not neglect the gift which is in you, [that special inward endowment which was directly imparted to you by the Holy Spirit]"* (1 Timothy 4:14 AM). If you are unaware of your gifts, abuse of them are almost unavoidable. The first step in living a purposeful life is to discover your natural endowments, which include anointings, gifts, callings, and talents. There is a reason and purpose God has blessed you with certain endowments. What are your special endowments? It could be singing, inventing, writing, healing, process technology, public speaking, caring for others, etc. The Greek words for gifts in I Peter 4:10 is translated charisma or divine gratuity or special endowment; something given by God that is not earned. The most common gift among us are listed in three primary passages in scriptures: I Corinthians 12, Ephesians 4:11 and Romans 12:6-8. Your endowments are significant tools to work and build on the path toward your destiny. These gifts of God are forms of creative energy to perform whatever tasks God created you to execute for His purpose and glory.

H (Heartbeat)

The **H** stands for Heartbeat because your heart is your divine instinct and the seat of intuition, prophetic intelligence, passion, inspiration, and drive that impulsively direct your steps. Also, the heart fuels the operation of your gifts by a soulical and heartfelt instinct. When you are born again and yield to Jesus' Lordship, it is the part of you that sounds like God's voice and functions as His microphone that speaks truth to your soul and body what is really true. It is that part of you that carries and sustains your yearning and energy on the route toward destiny. A healthy heart is the spring of a meaningful life; but a man with daily defeated impulses can never win. Proverbs 17:22 (NIV) says, *"A cheerful heart is good medicine, but a crushed spirit dries up the bones."* Just as the ear serves as an organ to hear audible sounds and help maintain balance in vertebrates, the heart is the inner ear through which you can connect with God and maintain your balance as you go through life. Your dreams and purpose get nourished or famished in your heart. Everything you do flows from it (Proverbs 4:23). Your heart operates your inward voice and inward witness to give you direction and clarity on a path toward destiny that is a direct route but not a straight line. What you hear speaking to you today is the true sound of God.

A (Ability)

The **A** represents Ability, the third factor in how you are SHAPED for the fulfillment of your purpose and destiny, which is an essential aspect of your destiny equation. Unlike Special Endowments, which flow naturally from within and from God, your ability is the strength or skills developed through training and experiences. Abilities and skills enable you to perform excellently in the purpose God has prepared for you. Without the strategic information and skills at your disposal to complement your gifts and limitation, your endowments and opportunities can go untapped. A man skillful in his work will stand among kings and not mean men (Proverbs 22:29). Joseph, for instance, was **SHAPED** for his purpose. He had the **Special Endowments** of dreaming (Genesis 35). His **Heartbeat** was kept healthy, and in alignment with the plan of God (Genesis 39), and over time, he developed a leadership ability through several **Experiences** and **Environments** that eased his path into **Destiny** and brought him before the king (Genesis 37). Gifts will open doors of destiny, but skills will give you profit in the fields and mountains of influence of your calling. Abilities and skills serve as multipliers enabling you with grace and charisma to consistently provide near-perfect performances of purpose and destiny with your God-given Endowments. You will be able to serve effectively and profitably while *Getting to the Other Side of* your *Through* (See Ecclesiastes 10:10).

P (Personality or Paradigms)

P is the Personality or Paradigm that gives us a unique lens through which we see the world and impulsive wiring to respond to life's elements. It serves as a pattern, predicator, or model for life and greatly influences what we are and become. David Funder defines personality as "a collection of relatively discrete, independent and narrow social capacities." It involves your character, temperament, disposition to life, worldview, etc. Your attitude determines your altitude. The way God has made you (personality) was determined by what He wants you to become. Our introvert and extrovert personality types are distinctively designed by God for relating to others. This helps us to function environmentally with those whom we are connected to impact them. Personality is routed in the origin of how God has wired us to hear from Him and act on His behalf. However, God wired you to relate to your world with either left-brain or right-brain dominant; not both. For example, a person who is left-brained is thought to be more logical, analytical, and objective. The person who is more right-brained is more holistic, artistic, innovative, and emotional. Brain dominance influences how we naturally relate to the natural and supernatural world. According to the theory of left-brain or right-brain dominance, each side of the brain controls different types of thinking. These two types of thinking are expressed in how individuals apply their purpose and destiny to life.

E (Experiences and Environments)

E is for Experiences and Environments that help you become what God has prepared for you. God, being the Potter and Maker, places us in an environment that is perfect for His plans for us and allows certain experiences to shape us for our destiny. Remember the story of Joseph, Moses, Daniel, David, etc. Even though God wanted to announce David to the world through his killing of Goliath, He first placed him in the wilderness where he learned to kill a lion and a bear (1 Samuel 17). The environment and experiences in your life are fundamental to how you are SHAPED and prepared for the future. The wilderness sometimes is the route to the Promised Land, and the dark valley can also lead to the sunlit hill and horizon. Your experiences should teach you life lessons, enhance maturity, and make you stronger while going through enjoyable and painful times. Experience can bring out the excellence of God in you, especially if you learn to handle situations with prayer, God's word, particularly bearing the fruit of the Spirit—love, joy, peace, longsuffering, kindness, goodness, faithfulness, gentleness, and self-control. Your environment should further enhance you on the journey towards the place of destiny. Myles Munroe says, "Purpose transforms mistakes into miracles and turns disappointments into testimonies." God does not see your past mistakes the way you see them. You might see a *mess*, but God sees a *message* and platform for miracles. "Many are the plans in a person's heart, but it is the LORD's purpose that prevails" (Proverbs 19:21 NIV). Regardless of what experience and environments have shaped you, it is the plan of God that prevails. We overcame by the blood of the lamb and the words of their testimony.

D (Destiny)

D is for Destiny—everything that will happen during our lifetime and in eternity, planned or unplanned. Yet, we are empowered to impact our destiny through the decisions and actions. Everything about the way we are SHAPED leads us to our Destiny. One thing we all have in common is that we have all come into the world with a purpose and a destiny, which is a direct route nut never a straight line. Our purpose is the overall reason why we are here, and there is no one born without a purpose. God says in Isaiah 46:10, "I have known the end from the beginning, from ancient times, what is still to come. I say, 'My purpose will stand, and I will do all that I please.'"

Finally, you have been SHAPED for an uncommon destiny. Never try to become someone else. You are uniquely designed for your destiny. What the Lord has made crooked, who can make straight? Walk in your purpose and destiny. You have charisma and gift to impact the world.

Dr. Daniel Haupt is a prophetic voice and Kingdomcentric teacher and destiny thought leader on the seven mountains of influence and host of the Voice of Destiny Show. To reach this author for speaking engagements, programs and services email him at drhaupt@voiceofdestiny.org.

To learn more about the author and upcoming OSOT itinerary go to osot.life.

Top Five Talents: Achiever, Learner, Input, Relator & Responsibility

Chapter 2

The pursuit of destiny

"Write the vision and make it plain on tablets, that he may run who reads it." – Habakkuk 2:2

By Dr. Paul Thornton

What is destiny to you? Depending on one's point of view, the term *destiny* can mean different things. For some, a person's destiny is described as everything that happens to them during his or her life, including what will happen in the future, especially when it is considered to be controlled by someone else. Some would define destiny as the predetermined, preordained, inevitable path for one's life considered as something beyond human power or control. Destiny is often considered an eternal call on the inside of someone based on a divine decree that keeps them focused and determined against all the odds. Some view destiny as that job, that business, that dream, that desire, that invention, or that divine word that is pursued with passion and determination. Others believe destiny is that ordained purpose for which one is created. It is that settled place in God that one has absolutely nothing to do with. Destiny is often referred to as that prearranged path that wakes a person up every day and motivates them to reach personal goals and make a difference in the world. No matter what one considers destiny to be, it is inspired by purpose.

When one is pursuing their purpose, he or she needs to realize there will be many challenges to face that will try to distract, discourage, and derail them from their predestined path. Life takes various turns, and not all paths are positive. As one avidly pursues their destiny, distractions can occur in the form of sickness, death of loved ones, financial struggles, family problems, personal issues, and the list goes on and on. Achieving a destiny of greatness is not an easy process. The pursuit of destiny is not a quick race but a lifelong marathon. For the marathon runner, the twenty-six-mile competition is not just a test of how fast they can run but their willingness to endure and persist until they reach the finish line. A marathon runner, while trying to reach for his goal, may endure bad weather conditions, muscular fatigue, dehydration, mental exhaustion, periods of agony, and the high cost of paying the price with blood, sweat, and tears.

When pursuing destiny, everyone wants the outcome before going through the process. Everyone wants the prize. Everyone wants the reward of reaching their dreams. Everyone wants to be a champion, but often, we do not want to go through what it takes to get there. *The other side of through* is the process that makes champion. Regardless of the individual path that has been assigned to each of us, there are two key qualities that are needed if a person is going to reach their destiny – endurance and persistence. These are two of the virtues needed to cross the finish line.

Endurance and Persistence

Endurance is the ability to bear unpleasant or difficult circumstances without giving way to the situation. Persistence is the ability to continue in the course of action, in spite of opposition. It is the ability to be determined to do or achieve something regardless of the setbacks. Persistence is the difference between a successful outcome and a failed one due to giving up. Major success seldom comes easy or without a great deal of effort. Often the only difference between those who succeed and those who don't, is the ability to keep going long after the rest have stopped pursuing their destiny. Developing endurance and persistence is a master skill for achieving destiny. It is easier to relax and do nothing or live in our comfort zone. It is relatively easy to persist when things are going well, and we see progress, but highly persistent people have found ways to keep going despite major setbacks and a lack of evidence that they are moving closer toward their goals.

When hit with any hardship or discouragement, it is difficult to know exactly what to do or which direction to take. There are several principles that can be applied to one's life to help endure and persist when pursuing their destiny. First, persistent people know what their purpose is. Many people do not know what their purpose is or what they want. One can find their purpose through the process of elimination. Focus on what you don't want and move those items out of your life. Once a person knows what he/she wants to do in life, it provides a sense of meaning and momentum to advance personally.

Second, persistent people recognize they have an all-consuming vision. Persistent people have a goal or vision in mind that motivates and drives them. They are often dreamers and visionaries who see their lives as having a higher purpose than simply earning a living. Their vision is deeply ingrained, and they focus on it constantly with great emotion and energy. Enduring people often think of their vision first when they wake up, and it is the last thing before they go to bed. Reaching their goal becomes the focal point of their life, and they devote a major portion of their energy and time toward reaching it.

Third, persistent people never look for an excuse or a way out. What keeps highly persistent people going is their powerful level of desire. Repeated failures, dead ends, and periods when it seems like no progress is being made, often come before any breakthroughs happen. Tenacious people have inner energy and intensity to keep themselves motivated and going through these tough times. People with the ability to endure have a good understanding of themselves, their situation, and are seldom swayed by the opinion of the masses.

Fourth, persistent people the ability and flexibility to adjust and adapt their action plan. They do not remain stubborn in the face of evidence that their plan is not working but look for better ways that will increase their effectiveness and chances of success. A person of endurance knows their journey may include a series of dead ends, detours, and adjustments but have complete faith that they will reach their final destination. They are not tied to their ego and are quickly willing to admit when something is not working. A person of endurance realizes that any goal worth reaching will take time, effort, and continuously learning new skills and thinking patterns. They welcome change, new ideas, and continue looking for ways they can incorporate these into their lives.

Fifth, persistent people understand that ongoing learning is seen as part of a process through which the highly resolute continually expand the range of tools they have to work with. Naturally curious, resolute types not only see learning a way of reaching their goals more quickly, but they also see self-development as a way of life. Learning and continual growth do not end at a certain age or stage of life, but they are the essence of life itself, and therefore never-ending.

Sixth, persistent people understand perception is in the eye of the beholder. If someone perceives their life in a negative way, then more than likely, they will deal with all of the emotions and thoughts that come from that perception. In other words, thinking negative thoughts—in any situation—is going to bring out negative emotions. This type of thinking can get one stuck in a tailspin, and he/she will find it very difficult to get past emotions such as anger, sadness, and low self-esteem, which go along with negative perceptions. Negative perceptions will ultimately hinder one's pursuit of destiny.

Seventh, persistent people know how to maintain their focus. One of the obstacles to attaining destiny is losing **motivation** and focus. A good way to maintain focus is to **visualize** oneself accomplishing their goals no matter what it takes. A person of endurance needs to vividly see themselves accomplishing their goals. They need to keep their eyes on the prize. People of endurance should avoid getting caught up in negative or unproductive thinking such as, "This will never work." or "I can't do this." Instead, keep inspiring slogans handy, stories of those who have persevered in life, and whatever else that will motivate and boost their drive to succeed.

Lastly, persistent people know how to create a strategy and take action. When a person has a positive attitude and is able to see the vision of where they want to be, this is the time to start filling in the details with a direction to start moving in. The key here is to make the decision to consciously move forward and have a solid action plan to follow. Ask yourself, "What are my next steps?" "Who are the people involved with my next phase?" and "Where am I headed?' As you are moving forward with your plans, make sure you surround yourself with people who care about you, want the best for you, and believe in you. If allowed, naysayers and negative people can drastically hinder your destiny's progress. I am personally familiar with all of these principles because I had to continually reflect upon and lean on them as I completed my doctoral journey.

My doctoral journey

In 2013, I was divinely inspired to return to school to get a Masters' degree in Management and Leadership. Going back to college was not something I had a personal desire for or was even remotely thinking about. Through the process of time, I found out that the educational journey I was about to embark upon was a major part of my purpose and destiny. Once I was done with the two-year Masters' degree program, I assumed that I was done with school. Again in 2015, I was divinely inspired to enter the Doctor of Strategic Leadership Program at Regent University. Between the masters' and doctoral programs, it was a tough six years. Even though I knew it was my destiny to complete the doctoral program, it was a very difficult and challenging time. It took a lot of persistence and endurance to complete it.

In 2016, during my second semester, I became extremely ill from a mission's trip and was hospitalized for several days. My recovery took approximately five months. It was hard for me to complete any of my assignments, but I remember the feelings of determination that I had to continue the journey. As a result of God's favor, my professors worked with me, and I was able to complete the semester on time, in spite of my health challenges. During my doctoral journey, I was not just going to school. I had the responsibilities of being a husband, a father, working a full-time job, and traveling in ministry. For six years without a semester break, I carried my textbooks and laptop with me everywhere I went. I would study, do research, and write papers while on the plane, at lunch during work, and in hotels between ministry meetings. There were countless days I was up to two and three o'clock in the morning studying, and I needed to be to work at 9:00 a.m. There were many times during the journey I could not spend time with my family or close friends because destiny required that I study.

What is the one thing that kept me going for six years? The pursuit of my divine call. I had instructions from God to complete the doctoral journey because my next phase of life depended upon it. There were so many days that I was physically and mentally exhausted, emotionally discouraged, and I wanted to quit. I wished for my wife to tell me to quit, so that I could be relieved of the constant pressure and stress. But God had already prepared my wife to walk the journey with me, in terms of her support and prayers. She would not allow me to quit. She would pray for me. Then, whatever distraction was occurring at that moment would lift, and I would return to my studies.

During my doctoral journey, I had to make a personal choice to endure and be steadfast. I had to choose to daily embrace God's purpose and plan for my life, even though I did not like the process. I had to choose to remain motivated and focused. I had to choose not to be distracted by life's winds and waves. I had to choose to endure the mental exhaustion and physical fatigue I was experiencing. I had to remain resolute beyond the comments of those who suggested I needed to slow down and quit because I was involved in too much.

In May 2019, I completed my doctoral journey. As difficult as it was, persistence and endurance were essential for my life, so that I could move on to my next level of destiny. Pursuing destiny will never be easy. Embracing purpose will always have its challenges. Following our passions will involve moments of frustration. But if the skills for persistence and endurance are properly developed, you will successfully cross the finish line.

References

Campbell, C. (2016); *The 12 Invaluable Lessons Learned Enduring Hardship and Stress;* retrieved from **https://www.entrepreneur.com/article/283967**.

Deutschendorf, H. (2015*); 7 Habits of Highly Persistent People*; retrieved from **https://www.fastcompany.com/3044531/7-habits-of-highly-persistent-people**.

Harmon, J. (2019); *How to Endure and Overcome the Worst of Life's Hardships;* retrieved from **https://www.lifehack.org/articles/communication/how-to-endure-and-overcome-the-worst-of-lifes-hardships.html**.

Macabasco, L. (2019); 6 *Effective Ways to Become Persistent*; retrieved from **https://www/lifehack.org/articles/productivity/6-effective-ways-to-become-persistent.**

Dr. Paul Thornton is an executive Life Coach and Seven Mountain Five-Fold Ministry gift. To reach this author for speaking engagements, programs and services email him at pwthornton@live.com.

To learn more about the author and upcoming OSOT itinerary go to osot.life.

*Top Five Talents: Input, Learner, Achiever, Connectedness &
Intellection*

Chapter 3

When your dream becomes a nightmare:
How to exit the nightmare and dream again

By Bishop, Rev. Dr. Sandra Hayden

"For a dream comes through much activity"
(Ecclesiastes 5:3 NKJV)

I started out with a beautiful dream. It was a dream I shared with
people I love and will always cherish. Now, I'm not talking about
the images, sensations, thoughts, and drama that play out while
we sleep. I'm referring to my hope for tomorrow, vision for the
future, and a strong desire that burned brightly within my heart. It
has never always been easy. I've found purpose in peril and
inspiration in life's process. Here is my story. I received the Lord
at a very young age. I grew up in church and did everything to
please the Lord. I didn't want to meddle with sin, so I got married
quite early. Growing up, I had always dreamed of being married,
having a family, and doing ministry. After we married, my

husband and I were both in ministry, and we were blessed with three wonderful children. Fortunately, some years later, the Lord called us to pastor a church, and without hesitation, we began serving God with joy and a deep sense of fulfillment. I was living my dreams! Unfortunately, a year after we moved into our new edifice, my husband passed away. Back then, I was 35 years old, and he was 43. It was like my world just collapsed suddenly without prior notice because my dream of enjoying a blissful marriage and doing ministry with my husband became a nightmare.

There was so much pain in my heart that I could not understand. I couldn't wrap my mind around the fact that God allowed such a tragedy to happen to me. I felt like a victim, and all that was left were shattered dreams. I questioned the Lord for quite some time. Why me? I asked, very often. I got frustrated because I couldn't figure out why. So, I had a lot of anger. I was angry with God. Even more, I was angry with my former husband because he left me. I felt abandoned. I felt like my husband had abandoned me, our children, and the ministry. It was as if he had control over his own death.

Where is God in our dreams?

You need to understand that God originally created us with a desire, passion, and purpose. There is also a connection between our dreams and His purpose for our lives. Although His purpose has more influence on us than our dreams and goals, really, He is the giver of them all.

Even though dreams flow out of purpose, they don't come before purpose. They are strategies to move us towards the ultimate plan of God for our lives. In my case, I believe I have a call of God on my life. It was God's ultimate purpose for my existence. Even though I didn't really want to answer that call, I was able to get myself in line with the call to serve in ministry through marriage. Actually, I still wanted to live out my own dream. I craved the love in marriage and the excitement of ministry while shying away from the true demands of the call.

Eventually, I found myself at a critical crossroads. I had to choose between my desires and God's plans for my life. Therefore, upon the home going of my husband, it dawned on me that I was either going to finally answer the call of God, or be stuck in a place of anger with God because the dream I once had was now a living nightmare.

During this dark time in my life, I learned that God is sovereign. He is good, wise, and always seeking to bless us. God loves us, and He always will, regardless of the hurt we might be going through.

I appreciate the fact that before I was formed, I was in God, and before I was in my mother, I was still in God. He sent me to the world to fulfill His purpose. All I'll always need is to trust Him in every situation.

It's not going to be a free ride

Coming to the point of surrender will always produce peace with God and progress in life. Yet, surrendering to God means standing against the enemy. God's plan will not always come to pass without an active pursuit!

Remember, I said, "I've been there!" So, believe me when I say: fulfilling a God-given dream will not be a walk in the park. Don't think that because your dream was from God, fulfillment is guaranteed. Indeed, your dream will try you at some point before it's finally fulfilled. For instance, consider Apostle Paul, when you read his writings about how he was stoned, beaten, and abused. It always seemed as though his dream was turning to a nightmare. However, he held on to His convictions and hope of glory. Even in suffering, Paul counted it all joy till he walked in the streets of Glory by the side of Jesus, whose gospel he had lived, believed, preached, and died for.

Also, Joseph had a dream. He woke up one morning with a dream to become a great leader. Sadly, this became his nightmare when his brothers hunted him and tried to drown his dreams in the pit of hate and mire of servitude. Unfortunately, the next few weeks after Joseph's dream, he was sold as a slave to Egypt. Even after things got a little better in Potiphar's house, he was eventually implicated and thrown into the dungeon. Fortunately, because Joseph never gave up, he rose to prominence, and His dream became a reality. His dream tried him till he became the perfect Prince for Egypt.

So, regardless of what you are going through, know that God has given you a dream. So, keep at it until it is fulfilled. Does it seem like things are falling in different directions? Does it seem like you are heading for a crash? Don't despair. Your dream was meant to be fulfilled, and it will be!

Rather than complain and give up when you go through some rough path while fulfilling God's plan for your life, look to the brighter side. It may seem as though it's already becoming a nightmare but can still hold on to your dream. Your victory will inspire people and provide hope, so don't give up!

On different occasions, I've heard many people say, *"Woman of God, when I look at your life, I was able to develop strength."* This is very special to me. When someone hears about everything that I have walked through in the past, it encourages them to continue in their walk with God today. For this, I'm eternally grateful.

In reality, God may allow an unpleasant experience in your life because He has to have an example. He needs an example of His power and glory. Don't panic! God will sustain you while you walk through the storms and through the fire. You will not be burned. Instead, you will come out on the other side of whatever your current situation may be.

Furthermore, challenges may eventually expose your inner weaknesses; yet, God is not seeking to embarrass you but to help you develop character. The good thing is, when people finally look at you, they'll see God in you. More so, people will see the strength and glory of God in your life. They'll feel the grace of

God on you, and it will encourage and reassure them, knowing that if you made it through, they can make it through, also.

Comforting others, even when hurting

For me, during those tragic periods, whenever I went before my children, I didn't break down or allow them to see me crying. No! I continued to encourage them because not only was I hurting, they were also hurting. In fact, they were dealing with the same anger and pain that I was experiencing at that time.

Likewise, the members of the church were hurting and in need of encouragement. So, I decided to consistently reject the temptation to stop serving the Lord in church. I made myself available to continuously encourage the people, inspiring them to keep on believing the word, and trusting God.

I continued in the work and the assignment that God had given me. I discovered my purpose even when I was in pain. I knew it was just a process, and I couldn't afford to get stuck. My strength came from knowing that things would eventually turn out for my good. And, bless God, they did. Here's the point: God needs an example to help somebody, somewhere who may be going through a situation like yours. Somebody will hear about how you held on tightly to that dream until you became victorious, and they'll be inspired to stand up and rise up! Therefore, because of you, people will fight for victory, move with power, and trust God again to fulfill the promises and prophesies in their lives.

How to dream again

Often, our nightmares come from things and circumstances that are clearly out of our control. However, I believe you can recover from any nightmare and dream again. Here are some of the strategies that helped me to walk out of the dark tunnels of despair, into the light of hope and life of victory.

1. **Live a life of worship.** My healing came as I laid before the Lord in worship. It became my lifestyle, to the point that when people look at me, they say, "My God, you don't age." I respond, "It's the presence of God. So I developed a consciousness of God through worship. A life of worship prevents you from complaining because God cannot help you if you are given to murmuring. God inhabits the praises of His people. So, when you tune in to a lifestyle of genuine worship, the devil gets confused and wonders if you are the same person going through this rough path.

2. **You've got to build a good relationship with God**. God desires to relate to you and me. The Bible says in Amos 3:3 (KJV), "Can two walk together, except they be agreed?" That word means to harmonize. Your journey will begin by accepting Jesus into your heart as your Lord and Savior. That is the first step to receiving help from God. For instance, if you don't see a doctor, he won't be able to help you. So, lasting healing will come to you through a relationship with God—your Healer. God shouldn't be limited to an option in your life if you desire to rescue your dreams from nightmares.

3. **Learn to spend time in His presence**. Scheduling time to study the word and to pray must be a top priority on your to-do list. When God has no place in your day, He will have little power in your life. And when you get in the presence of God, pour out yourself in prayers. So, whatever pain you're in, whatever trauma you have experienced, God can bring healing to your heart and help you to renew your mind. However, as you praise and worship God everywhere and at all times, even with the hurt, you are inviting God into the situation. When Paul and Silas sang and praised God in chains, the foundation of the prison was literarily shaken, and their shackles were broken in pieces. Indeed, praise can set you free to move forward to fulfillment.

4. **Encourage your heart in the Lord**. This means talking to your heart. I'll explain. You see, when my husband passed on, and I was in pain, I would have to talk to myself and

encourage my own heart that God was going to bring me out of that situation. I had to remind myself of the things that God has already written about me because He's already written it in His word about me and about my purpose and destiny. So I went back to the scriptures to remind myself. So, what did God say to you? Go back to that book where you probably wrote it and constantly tell yourself that it will come to pass regardless of what you are going through.

5. **Be Patient and Forgive yourself**. Sometimes all we need is to be patient with God and even with yourselves. God is eternal. That is, He is outside of time. He created time, but He not limited by it. Understand that even though some things don't happen overnight, they will happen. The timing of God and the things of God don't happen overnight. I understand that we are in an age in which people want everything NOW! We want to be changed, healed, and transformed in an instant. However, it's not that God is not going to do it, but you need to understand the time factor involved in it. Furthermore, you need to forgive yourself. Let the pain go, knowing you can't undo the past. So forgive and grow in grace. That is the process of recapturing a new dream after several failed attempts in the past.

6. **Seek God's plan for your life**. One day, the Lord Jesus spoke to me. He said, *"I came that my people may have life, and have it more abundantly" (John 10:10)*. Still, many of them don't know how to live life. The problem is, most people have their own dreams, and they live out their entire lives on their own terms without ever finding out what is God's dream for them. Furthermore, God sent us here with a purpose and an intention for our lives. Therefore, we need to understand the purpose of God and His original intention for your life. So, if your dreams have been shattered, it's always good to go back to God for clarity of purpose. You will be reignited by your discovery.

7. **Don't disconnect from people**. As I traveled to different places, especially Africa, I was able to connect with people

and cultures that really helped me on my journey to recovery. They encouraged me to dream again. My trips to Africa allowed me to see men and women who were hungry for God. I saw the supernatural powers of God in Africa. I saw blind eyes open and limbs grow out in Guyana, which totally changed my life. It stirred my desire to know God in a deeper dimension. I started having a greater hunger to know God through my connection with people who burned with a dynamic love for Him.

A special encounter

On one instance, while I was returning from Africa, right there on the plane, I said, *"Oh God, I'm tired! I don't want anybody to sit next to me."* So I put my purse on the seat. Suddenly, a lady came and sat just next to me. I decided to turn my back on her, so I didn't have to even look at her. Then, the Lord said, "Turn and look her in the eyes." So, when I eventually turned and looked that lady in the eyes, I could see her pain. My God!

Well, the good news is, I ended up ministering to that lady after she told me the story of how her husband divorced her for someone else following 25 years of marriage. Upon getting off the plane, the lady grabbed me, and we stood together for a while. She was holding me so tight; people were beginning to stare. As those tears streamed down her face, I heard the Lord say to me, *"You see, your life is not your own."*

Glory to God! I dreamed again!

The great news is, God finally brought me out of the dark tunnel of nightmare and shattered dreams. He gave me another chance to love again and the courage to dream again, after all the perils of my past. I am currently married to Gregory Hayden, with whom I'm fulfilling God's dream and purpose for my life.

In conclusion, don't give up! The Bible says, the clay was marred, but the Potter never stopped working with the clay. Hmmm! Don't you see it? Even with marred clay, the potter kept believing. Well, the truth is, God is the potter, and you are the clay. So, why would you stop believing when God won't stop working?

God Bless You!

Dr. Sandra Hayden has a unique ministry as evidenced by the manifestations of healings, salvation of souls, miracles and the abundance of financial prosperity throughout her over 30 years in ministry. She is the founder of the Apostolic Alliance, an organization of Sixteen churches & ministries committed to addressing the needs of the Senior leadership and other five-fold ministry gifts.

To reach this author for speaking engagements, programs and services email her at bishopatwork@aol.com.

To learn more about the author and upcoming OSOT itinerary go to osot.life

Chapter 4

The phenomenal family:
Going through shocking adversity with victory

Inspired by The Voice of Destiny Talk Show, Featuring Gary and Sharon Worrell

The family is not just a basic unit of the society, consisting of the husband, wife, and children, it is a platform instituted by God for humans to perfectly fulfill their divine destinies. It is not a legal or traditional contract of companionship, nor an act of cohabiting as it is often seen. Rather, it is the physical and spiritual connection of two different and imperfect lives to become one. Dr. Myles Munroe in *The Purpose and Power of Love and Marriage,* defines marriage as the coming together of "two imperfect people, committing themselves to a perfect institution, by making perfect vows from imperfect lips before a perfect God." *"And the LORD God said, 'It is not good that man should be alone; I will make him a helper comparable to him."* (Genesis 2:18 NKJV). Adam, like every other person on earth today, was created with a specific purpose in the heart of God. However, on the path to his destiny, God saw that he needed the combined energy of a partner for him not to crash out as he journeys into his ordained purpose. Hence, He gave him a wife and therefore established the family as a fundamental condition for life's accomplishment.

From the beginning of time, the phenomenal family has been a formidable instrument in the hand of God to expand His glory on earth. By phenomenal family, we mean a family with years of encouraging testimonies and consistent victories over several difficulties that come with marriage. A person's destiny is often determined by the kind of family or background he/she is coming from. A confused marriage will ultimately lead to a confused life, while a progressive home will make progressive individuals. No wonder it appears as if many sweet love stories are leading to heartbreaks, and many marriages are ending in divorce. It appears as if the enemy of the Church is stirring the storm of crises in the home to distract men and women from becoming who they are created to be. Studies have shown that about 58 to 62 percent of marriages and about 40 percent of Christian marriages end in divorce. The family, in the original plan of God, is to be enjoyed and enabling, not to be endured and endangering. Why these terrible statistics of divorce? Why are homes splitting up by the day? Sincere expectations, even among believers, are ruined, the hopes of many heartbroken couples are dashed, and glorious destinies are aborted.

Every one of us has a destiny and purpose that is a direct route, but not a straight line. In order to adapt and leverage on the blessing of a phenomenal family, which is the will of God for us, we must remember stories like the Worrell's to remind us that everything works together for our good as we journey towards our destinies. Below is a wonderful testimony of a couple, who through the grace of God, have not only survived several crises but have also been able to translate those challenges encountered in their marriage into a source of strength to fulfill the mandate of God over their lives.

The true testimony of Gary and Sharon Worrell from the other side of through

"We've been married for 31 years, and we've been very blessed with the capability to go through a lot of difficult times. We've had difficult addictions, financial trouble, and moved multiple times in our marriage as we sought God on how He wants to design our home. By 2002, we had been married 19 years and that was when we experienced one of our greatest setbacks. I (Sharon) got a phone call from a Denver jail. I picked up the phone and it was Gary (my husband) who said he had been arrested. I was alarmed because, we were Christians; we go to church, we'd met in the church and all our activities revolved around the church. I asked him what he was arrested for and his reply was "it's all a big mistake, but it was for soliciting a prostitute." My world crashed on that day. It was like the man that I knew died. It was just an alarming thing, and quite seriously, nobody in the church could help me because nobody in the church knew what to say or how to go about even addressing it. It actually thrust us into the wilderness in such a way that we had to find a path to figure out what was going on. I seriously thought about divorcing Gary. I prayed and asked God what to do and if I was released from the marriage? One night, about a week after this had happened, I heard God tell me not to quit my marriage. I was very upset but felt like God was speaking to my heart and saying He wanted me to stay in this marriage. That in itself was alarming to me as well. I was going to stay in the marriage with conditions for recovery. My decision set us into motion on a journey with counsellors and people who could educate us about what sexual addiction is and help us understand how to proceed and attain recovery. What I came to realize is that Gary had led a perfect double life for 19 years. I soon discovered it was something that started when he was only eight years old. He was introduced to pornography, and that progressed into the addictive and deceptive lifestyle he led. That was a critical stage in our marriage. However, through the grace of God and the agency of helpful people around us, we didn't only come out strong, we have also been able to use that experience to help more lives and bless many families today."

The story of Gary and Sharon reveals that a wonderful marriage is not always devoid of crises and difficulties. Even Christian homes are not exempted from this. As you journey with your partner on the route of destiny, you might come to such crossroads where you have to walk carefully and make wise decisions; otherwise, it might degenerate into a very messing and unpleasant affair. Sexual addiction threatened to destroy the family of Mr. and Mrs. Gary Worrell. What is the story and state of your home? Maybe the challenge you are dealing with in your home is internet addiction, frequent misunderstanding, lack of commitment, etc. Do you know that there are no such things as perfect marriages anywhere? Even in the perfect world (the Garden of Eden), the first marriage officiated by God Himself and attended by the host of heaven still had its own trying times. Remember, in Genesis 3:1-23, how the serpent took advantage of the Eve's weakness to derail her home from the path of destiny. She, being deceived by the serpent, proceeded to persuade her husband to eat from the forbidden tree. This action cost them not just the pleasures of Eden but the very presence of God. Instead of obtaining the promise, they were cursed and condemned to a lifetime of hardship and pains, which must be transferred across all generations. However, even under the weight of the consequences of this difficulty, Adam wouldn't say to Eve (his wife), "You evil woman, get out of my life!" Rather, we read in Genesis 4:1 how they pulled through and became better as a married couple. Furthermore, there are no two perfect couples. In the first marriage, Eve was the weaker one, while in the case of Gary and Sharon, Gary was weaker. For Gary, his early exposure to pornography caused him to develop a sexually addicted lifestyle that eventually shook his marriage and home in later years. Your spouse or fiancé has a different background, life experience, and an already formed attitude that he/she is bringing into the marriage. These contrasting lifestyles might result in constant conflicts in the home and if not appropriately handled, can degenerate into a more complicated trouble and can ruin the family setting and purpose. Many homes have been broken, many good people have been traumatized, and many great destinies have been truncated as a result of the inability or unwillingness to pull through such trying times. Now, the question is, what do we do when experiencing such trying moments in our homes? There are times we may feel too weak, broken, and unmotivated to continue. Sharon, for example, admitted that she contemplated divorce. However, the conflict in her marriage did not lead her to the court filing for divorce but to the presence of God and to a counselor, seeking a solution and a way forward. When we come to such stumbling crossroads, we need God, the Originator of marriage, to help us. King Solomon counseled (in

Proverbs 3:5-8 NKJV), *"Trust not in your heart, and lean not on your own understanding. In all your ways acknowledge Him, and He shall direct your paths. Do not be wise in your own eyes; fear the LORD and depart from evil. It will be health to your flesh, and strength to your bones."* Because your eyes are set on a bright future, you cannot afford to travel through this perilous world alone. You need God to direct your steps and lead you in the right path. Sharon Worrell sought the face of God, and her testimony is enduring and edifying the world today. No matter how low you have fallen, with God, that valley can become a springboard that will launch you into unimaginable heights of glory. Seeking God's help in times of trouble should involve coming to the throne of grace in sincerity and repentance. In the words of Gary Worrell, "God wants to get us free from whatever the addiction is; whether it be sexual addiction or other areas. Let's be honest, it's repentance, making a 180-degree turn." Proverbs 28:13 (NIV) says, *"whoever conceals their sins does not prosper, but the one who confesses and renounces them finds mercy."* We can also read in 2 Peter 3:9 (NIV) that *"The Lord is not slow in keeping His promise, as some understand slowness. Instead He is patient with you, not wanting anyone to perish but everyone to come to repentance."* There is still balm in Gilead (Jeremiah 8:22 KJV). "Upon mount Zion, there shall be deliverance, and holiness; and the house of Jacob shall possess their possession" (Obadiah 1:17 KJV). You need not stay defeated when God has given you victory by paying the ultimate price for your liberty. So, use your liberty where it counts most—helping and working together with family.

According to Letty Cottin, "if the family is a boat, it would be a canoe that makes no progress unless everyone paddles." If you hope to tread the path of greatness into the fulfilment of God's plan over your marriage, you must walk and work with your spouse and other good people that encourage you in the right direction. Gary Worrell observed that isolating and disconnecting physically and emotionally from your spouse or other good people is a trap for destruction in marriage. When we withdraw from places where people can easily question the healthiness of our actions and decisions, it becomes very easy to venture into prostitution, alcoholism, gambling, drugs, gluttony, pornography, etc. and form an addictive attitude from it.

In the words of Mr. and Mrs. Gary Worrell; "It is easy to get deliverance. It is not just as easy to stay delivered." It helps to remember that there are advantages in staying together. *"Two are better than one, because they have a good return for their labor. For if one falls down, his companion can lift him up; but pity the one who falls without another to help him up... though one may be overpowered by another, two can withstand him. And a threefold cord is not quickly broken"* (Ecclesiastes 4:9-10, 12 9 (NKJV). Apostle James counseled in James 5:16 (NKJV) that you should *"confess your sins to each other and pray for each other so that you may be healed. The power of a righteous man has great power to prevail."* Although Sharon was deeply hurt, she was a supportive and helpful wife to her husband at that critical stage, and for over 30 years, they are still growing and getting stronger in love and in fulfilment of their purpose. This, we must admit, is an incredible and uncommon feat in this dispensation. Their marriage was not always perfect. In fact, they came to the same bridge that has ended many homes and families, and they survived by the grace of God.

Finally, we will conclude with the words of Charles Swindoll; "Focus on your marriage. Because that's the nucleus of the home, whatever you do to restore its health and strength will naturally restore what's broken among the other relationships." Your marriage is not destined for failure. God wants to see your family prospering on the path of destiny. Yield to God in repentance, follow Him in obedience, and He will lead you to the place of perfect peace and safety. Amen.

Top Five Talents: Developer, Deliberative, Connectedness, Relator &
Empathy

Chapter 5

My real life: The reality of a widow queen

By Juanita Y. Harris

"Real life comes by feeding on every word of the LORD"
(Deuteronomy 8:3b NLT). "But by every word that proceedeth
out of the mouth of the LORD doth man live" (Deuteronomy 8:3b
KJV). *"And real life comes by obeying every command of God"*
(Deuteronomy 8:3b LB).

Life continues after the death of the flesh. Not only do I believe
the Bible that says we will have eternal life, if we believe in our
Lord Jesus Christ, but my life continued after my husband went
home to be with the Lord. Although we were one, going through
the grief process can take years and can be very emotionally
painful.

BUT GOD!

After the death of my husband, my reality was altered by the REAL life of a widow. Reality was, I didn't have a special someone to come home to after my active life of serving the Lord. The only person I was responsible for was myself. For nine years, my youngest daughter and her children lived with me, and that was a blessing for all of us. Not being alone in the first years was what I needed. The children gave me a reason to get out of bed every morning as their mother went off to work, and they needed to get to school. Continuing my activities at church also gave me purpose. Even a little Yorkie named Tucker became a part of my reality. He wasn't someone I had ever thought I wanted in my life, but he because a big part of it. Who would have thought I would be spoiling a dog by heating his food in the microwave? It's amazing the things that affect our lives as we transition from one part of the journey to another. Now, I understand how people can love their pets. Tucker could never replace my husband or family, but he gave unconditional love, no matter how many times I told him to go away or accidentally stepped on him.

As the grandchildren reached their teen years and no longer needed my help, they became their own persons, which was not the way I was brought up. I began to desire more alone time away from the clamor of teen music and games on the television. So, when an opportunity presented itself, I packed up and moved out of my house to a condo. I left my daughter, the children, and the dog. For whatever reason, I needed time alone at that point in my journey.

My real life was living alone, which some days were good. Perhaps this was a transitional period to prepare me for the time alone I would have for almost three years. When alone, one can be honest about the feelings he/she is experiencing—hurt, anger, lust, loneliness, depression, joy, peace, compassion, love, and commitment. When one is alone, there is no distraction from another person to prevent you from looking deeply into your own feelings and emotions. There is no one to "make you mad." You can become angry with yourself, but that doesn't feel so good.

Consequently, I became more honest with me and God. He spoke to the things in me that had been hidden for decades. Some things were not pretty to look at — some things needed to be strengthened and made solid.

I was blessed to have received good biblical teaching and spiritual guidance, which helped me tremendously. I'm grateful GOD led my husband and I to a church in Virginia that gave us a firm spiritual foundation. Reconciliation Community Church in Virginia, under the leadership of Pastor John R. Peyton, gave us a well-rounded experience in the Lord Jesus Christ. We learned, prayed, worked, and loved. No, it was not a perfect church, but we were reminded often that the church belonged to Jesus Christ and He was the head. After we moved to Ohio, GOD led us to yet another church, Greater Grace Temple Church (GGT), under the leadership of then Pastor, and now Bishop Ronald M. Logan. We were going to visit other churches but never seemed to get around to doing it. That let me know we were at the church GOD intended for us. When I think of the other churches I could attend, there is no desire to leave GGT. We are not perfect, but family. Just like my natural family, not perfect, but I love them for who they are and for the love they show me.

After hours away from home, sometimes I just wanted to come home and vegetate. There were times when it would have been nice to have that significant other to tell about the highs and lows of my day; someone who would hug me just because I'm me; someone who has an interest in the whole person of me. Sounds a bit self-centered, but we need another human or more honestly other humans to be a part of our lives.

Emotions have been controlled by my reality. I've been angry that I had no one to help me organize or make major decisions. I wish my best sister/friend was not over 300 miles away or that my siblings were closer. For many years, my husband and children were enough, but now, it would be nice to visit with a sister or cousin more often. I'd like to spend a couple of weeks with my Aunt Catherine.

Sometimes being alone is wonderful and I'm happy to get home to an empty house. My house is my sanctuary of peace. Of course, I miss my husband and family. When I look at his pictures, sometimes there's a smile, and other times there may be tears. Because I don't want to feel the hurt of my husband's absence, I choose not to memorialize him on every occasion.

I remember, for sure, our anniversary, his birthday, my birthday, holidays, milestones in our children and grandchildren's lives, as well as my own milestones. How I would like to share so many things with him. But there are always memories, and that is a plus of being married and spending so many years together with the same person. You can create lots of good memories — the birth of our children, trips, holidays and the obstacles you overcame together.

Actions are a result of my emotions. Stress because I'm overwhelmed means I'm short-tempered or feeling down. When I feel down, I don't want to do anything or see anyone. Being alone gives me the energy to face the next challenge, which may be something as simple as making a phone call.

Other times, being with others lifts my spirit, and I'm ready to take on the world. Go figure, human nature and actions can't always be figured out. That is why only GOD knows our hearts. We don't even fully know ourselves.

Anger may come from hurt or fear. Try to see the reason for anger. A hurt person may express themselves with anger to keep from feeling the pain of the hurt. Crying out for help in our anger might be the action you see, but the emotion behind the anger, calls for compassion.

Learning to control our emotions, hence our actions will then help our healing process. Allowing emotions to provoke actions that may lead to sin will only make us more miserable in the long run.

Learning to allow others to know me better, rather than stifling my feelings was a part of my spiritual maturity. Forgiving those I love, has allowed me not to be angry about their actions. Realizing this, in our later years, my husband and I learned to forgive each other every day. Living with someone, when you both are "a piece of work," requires a great deal of forgiveness, no matter how much you love each other. My husband often saved me from myself because he knew me so well and could be honest with me when I was off track. Sometimes he would ask me, "Where is your faith?" I, in turn, could speak to his anger in indirect ways like frustrating slow drivers or someone not following the rules to the letter.

Love does cover a multitude of sins. As GOD loves us, let us work toward loving others.

The love of family and sister/friends has kept me over the years. The love of GOD sustains me daily. He shows me He loved me first and continues to love me, in spite of my mistakes and not showing Him the love and commitment He so deserves. But because He loves me unconditionally, He accepts my repentance and my "I'm sorry." His grace and mercy added to the love He shows me, overwhelms my heart sometimes. How can I not worship and praise my GOD?

Love a person, not their actions or attitude. Forgive those who don't understand your pain. Forgive those who cause you pain. Don't let your emotions trick you into thinking the wrong thoughts and cause you to act in an ungodly way. These are some of the ways to make it through those days when we just don't know what is wrong, but know we are not happy.

My own pain caused me to be more aware of others' pain and to be more compassionate toward them, even when I didn't understand their actions and did not approve of their behavior. More and more, I say, "But for the grace of GOD, there goes I." I could have used alcohol or drugs to ease the pain life had dealt me. I could be in a mental facility in deep depression. I could be in prison because I allowed my emotions to drag me into actions that are illegal and immoral.

Emotions can trick you into thinking the wrong thoughts and cause you to act in an ungodly way. As scripture says, *"Casting down imaginations, and every high thing that exalteth itself against the knowledge of God, and bringing into captivity every thought to the obedience of Christ"* (2 Corinthians 10:5 KJV). I'm sure I was not in my right mind after my husband passed away. I'm so grateful for my church family in Virginia and my new family in Ohio. They kept me looking up to GOD, who has sustained me for almost thirteen years.

Every time I read in the Bible how much GOD loves the widow, the orphan, and the poor, I'm so encouraged. Also, I love His commitment to be a husband to the widow. There can be no better husband than the LORD Himself.

Juanita Harris is a professional life coach, Christian counselor and prison ministry leader with a special message for those who have been made widows by God and those who have been made widows by man.

To reach this author for speaking engagements, programs and services email her at juanitah2000@yahoo.com.

To learn more about the author and upcoming OSOT itinerary go to osot.life.

Chapter 6

P.R.I.D.E.: Steps for taking charge of your destiny

Inspired By "The Voice of Destiny" Radio Show, featuring Dr. Felix Gilbert

... "walk worthy of the calling with which you were called." –
Ephesians 4:1 NKJV

Have you ever awakened one day and realized you are in the middle of nowhere? Do you feel lost in the crowd as you continue to seem invisible in plain sight? Are you depressed and frustrated, feeling like there has to be more to life than mere survival, just existing and passing time? Do you think there is something you just might be missing? Are you feeling stuck and alone, lost and disconnected, constantly living behind the shadow of your true self? And finally, are you losing a sense of inner power and personal responsibility for your journey?

Well, if your answer to any of these questions is yes, then you need to keep reading. I'm writing to those who are tired of self-pity, the blame game, and hopeless reliance on other persons or things for the outcome of their lives. I believe it is time we realize that, with God, excellence, and a higher standard is attainable. Everyone has a purpose and a destiny to fulfill in life. Everyone was created by God and sent to the earth with a clear intention and a divine purpose.

Nobody is on this side of heaven just because Momma got pregnant. There are overwhelming biological and spiritual proofs that you and I are here only because God already had a special place for us to not just survive but to thrive and flourish.

There is a question in this world that has its answer with you and you alone. There are global problems for which God has put the solutions inside you. Do you believe this? I am emphatically telling you there are great and precious endowments in you that are yet to be explored, fervently awaiting expression.

However, the purpose and destiny we have been called to fulfill is a direct route and not a straight line. There are obstacles and different circumstances on our path to fulfilling purpose in life. Overcoming these obstacles is referred to as the Other Side Of Through (OSOT). Here is the all-important question: how can you overcome life's challenges and still arrive at that great destination, without aborting your divine destiny, in spite of all the obvious setbacks and subtle restraining forces? If this sounds like a question you need an answer to, then continue reading this chapter.

Furthermore, you are sure to reach your destination as you navigate life, if you take P.R.I.D.E or elements of personal responsibility in all you do. Here what the acronym P.R.I.D.E stands for.

Personal Responsibility - i.e., responsibility for using your potentials.

Relationship - responsibility for how you relate to God, your enemies, and those around you.

Interdependence - responsibility for working with others to use your potential to get to destiny.

Destiny and Development - making use of what God has given you right where you are on the ladder of progress.

Excellence - doing all of these with moral excellence and high standards.

Therefore, the acronym, P.R.I.D.E. is all about taking personal responsibility to lead with the level of excellence that is necessary to efficiently navigate life and arrive at that place of glory, manifestation, and high performance that God has already prepared.

The spiritual warfare to be applied is based on the fact that, whenever the enemy does or says anything that defies God's plan for your life, as a believer, you have the power, authority, and an obligation to take personal responsibility for overcoming. Believing and knowing this, you can deliver excellent results or accomplishments.

Moreover, our premise of taking P.R.I.D.E. in life's situations primarily finds its firm roots in the historical encounter between David and Goliath as narrated in the Bible. When the army of Israel was being bullied by the giant Philistine warrior, Goliath, David took responsibility personally, confronting him, man-to-man. David was bold because of his relationship with God. Yet, he was only able to challenge the enemy due to King Saul's permission because he was not an official member of Israel's army. David developed his skill from killing lions and bears, to a giant champion warrior. He applied an unusual but excellent strategy for defeating the "uncircumcised Philistine." (Read 1 Samuel 17:21-51) I believe we can learn from these principles and just take P.R.I.D.E. for the same victory in our lives.

At this juncture, let's go through these principles, one after the other, and further examine how they apply to your life, so you can also start taking P.R.I.D.E. for consistent triumphs in life.

Personal Responsibility

How far can one go in a world that teaches us to be dependent, a culture that just wants to constantly give us fish and bread rather than teach us how to get it ourselves? A lot of times, we find it difficult to break loose from such a suppressive mentality. Most people seem comfortable with taking a stand under an already erected canopy. I believe we must never attempt to engage the enemy against our advancement in life by mindlessly flowing in someone else's path, power, or anointing. You are not designed to use somebody else's stuff; you've got what it takes to move your life forward!

When you try to float with somebody else's talent and anointing, you will not have the required confidence, security, and boldness necessary to engage the enemy in spiritual warfare and win. So then, it becomes imperative and essential that you know who you are in Christ, the sets of gifting, tools, and or resources that God has given you, if you are going to engage the enemy and take P.R.I.D.E.

For instance, looking at the story of David while he was preparing to confront Goliath, Saul tried to place his own personal armor on David. But when David tried it on, it didn't fit him, so he was smart enough to take it off. He was an expert in using a sling shot and smooth stones, free of heavy armor.

On the contrary, here's what some people do in the world today. They try to engage the enemy based on what they see others do and don't realize that they are their own individual priests. God has uniquely anointed and gifted each person to do the things that He's called him or her to do. Lack of understanding of your purpose will make you act out the gift of others, thereby exposing yourself to abuse.

Everyone has a gift that is uniquely given by God to accomplish a creative purpose on the earth. God told Jeremiah in Jeremiah 1:5 KJV, *"Before I formed thee in the belly I knew thee; and before thou camest forth out of the womb, I sanctified thee, and I ordained thee a prophet unto the nations."* Each one of us was uniquely created by God to do a unique thing because God would not just create you and release you in the world with no purpose. So, embrace this mental awareness, and it will help to position you for success. Sometimes the problem is, we start seeing gifts of others that seem more prominent and recognized.

Avoid comparing yourself with others because there is nobody like you. I admonish you, take P.R.I.D.E. by taking personal responsibility to discover your purpose. The reason you are admiring others is that they probably went to God in prayer, petitioning Him to lead them in the path of His purpose for their lives. Many people are waiting for you to take P.R.I.D.E and find out where you belong. And when you do, stay focused, cultivate your gifts, and watch yourself grow. But all these require the components of P.R.I.D.E.

Relationship

This refers primarily to building a solid relationship with God, which will impact your relationship with those around you. It is important to know that taking P.R.I.D.E can be very fruitless if you don't know God. Daniel gave an assurance of the outcome of seeking to know God more. He said such people shall be strong, and they shall do exploits (Daniel 11:32). In other words, they shall command extraordinary accomplishments. So, it calls for an intimate relationship with God; that personal walk with Him; the sense of always seeking and hearing from God for direction and guidance. And this relationship must be genuine. It can't be fake nor superficial. This most important relationship is either platonic or plastic. There's no game playing.

I love the way David describes his relationship with God, this cannot be a surface fellowship, it runs deep. *"My soul longeth, yea, even fainteth for the courts of the LORD: my heart and my flesh crieth out for the living God"* (Psalms 84:2). So again, taking P.R.I.D.E. means your relationship with God must be authentic. This simply happens by talking to, listening, and hearing, then obeying Him. Just take some time and get to know Him.

Interdependence

This talks about two or more, depending on something or each other. We are all members of one body, and no one body can function perfectly well without the involvement of all the members being healthy. We need each other; everybody has a critical role within the body of Christ and in the world. And so, when it comes to identifying our gifts, we just have to go to God, spend time in the presence of our Father, cry out to God, saying, "God reveal to me who you are." Don't be afraid. Because even after we are sure of the gift, we still allow fear to stop us from expressing the gift of God. We still need the body (fellow brothers and sisters) to affirm the gifts that we have. We all need love and support. For instance, when I use my gifts, there's going to be affirmation from the people that I'm serving. This is because the gifts and anointing are given to serve God and people and bring glory to His name.

Destiny and Development

Consider, in light of your gifts, skills, and talents, where has God positioned you? How can you use these valuable personal assets where you are, to get to where you desire? And most importantly, how do you get to where God desires you to be? Once you search and begin finding answers to these questions, you are intentionally pursuing destiny. Also, in taking P.R.I.D.E., we should understand the place of focus in doing what God has destined for us to do. Nothing meaningful will be achieved without a life of focus. Another question is, what has God committed into your hand? What is that area of gifting that you have discovered about yourself? Understand, there is an intentional work that God needs to accomplish using that gifting. Sometimes we can get confused and miss what God is trying to do in and through us. It can be easy to overlook the fact that God has positioned us in a particular location, at a particular ministry, at a particular time, to do the things that He has called us to do. Even that place, which is in the will of God for us, may not look and feel like we think it should. Know that whatever challenges we face there, perceived as positive or negative, will work to our good. Therefore, we must be cognizant of our current environment, so we don't miss the opportunity that God has there for us.

Also, please understand the signal of God per time; when He is done with us in a particular place, He will create circumstances to begin to shift us to that next place of assignment. This is because God has an itinerary for each of us on our journey to destiny.

Excellence

This means the quality of been outstanding and extremely good. Excellence should be a way of life, not your behavior, when things are well. For instance, Joseph had walked through the situations and circumstances that he had to navigate on the way to his destiny. While in prison, he took P.R.I.D.E. While in Potiphar's house, he took P.R.I.D.E. I mean, while in the pit, he still took P.R.I.D.E. So, wherever Joseph found himself, he took personal responsibility to deliver the excellence that was necessary for his destiny. Consequently, God prospered the house of Potiphar and the prison because of Joseph.

Excellence is extremely important to the heart of God as it relates to who He made us to be. So don't settle for doing anything half way because it is not pleasing to the sight of God. We serve an excellent God. We serve a God that's spared nothing but to give us His best. Matter of fact, He didn't give a second servant, He gave us Himself in the form of His son to come and die in our place.

And a lot of times, when it comes to us serving God, we don't give our all but will give the world our very best. We give our places of employment the very best we can give them. But then when it comes to giving to God, some say, "Oh, just serve the Lord, never desiring to go to that next level with God.

When Solomon was building the temple of God, he put the best into it. Furthermore, as children of God, let's exemplify excellence in our character, excellence in our behavior, and excellence in our interaction with each other. Be the same at home and in public. Change inconsistent, shaky behavior into consistent, reliable character and integrity. Put the culture of excellence in all that you do; in your relationship with people, in your interactions, in business, the way you dress, and especially in the way you raise your children and influence grandchildren. Model an excellence mentality before them.

Finally, excellence really is the moral nature of God. God is an excellent God. Observe the synergy of how He created this planet, made the plant and animal kingdoms with precision and balance in nature. There was an excellent distinction about that. Study the intricate dynamics of the DNA system; how it records, reports, and preserves hereditary traits, passed down through every generation. God is so excellent in his work. This is who God is and we to be and function like our Heavenly Father.

Top Five Talents: Futuristic, Discipline, Restorative Focus & Achiever

Chapter 7

Finding identity and purpose in Christ

By Destiny Haupt

"Therefore, if anyone is in Christ, he is a new creation, old things have passed away; behold, all things have become new." –
2 Corinthians 5:17 NKJV

In order to fully understand your identity and purpose in Christ, you must know what they both mean from a biblical standpoint. From the beginning of time, God had planned what He wanted us humans to live for, but because of sin and the fall people have lost their relationship with God, hearing His voice. Consequently, there is an identity crisis. We latch on to whatever the culture, flesh, sin habits, iniquity, and other influences tell us to do. The world is in chaos, and God sent Jesus to the world to restore and redeem the damage made by sin and the devil. Jesus is the missing piece to the puzzle. One of my favorite books in the world, the Bible, reflects our mess, shows us who we really are without God, and gives us a beautiful picture of who God intended us to be and our value.

Our identity is linked directly to God and exceeds the usual definitions. The meaning of identity according to the Webster dictionary is the distinguishing character or personality of an individual, the condition of being the same with something described or arrested, and sameness of essential or generic character in different instances. These meanings are useful but not sufficient. When God created humans, He gave man and woman a unique identity, a carbon copy of Himself with instructions for His "product" as Dr. Myles Monroe says in his book titled, *In the Pursuit of Purpose.*

Let's start with identifying a few scriptures that speak on identity. Then God said, *"Let us make mankind in our image, in our likeness, so that they may rule over the fish in the sea and the birds in the sky, over the livestock and all the wild animals, and over all the creatures that move along the ground"* (Genesis 1:26-27 NIV). In this verse, I believe the Holy Spirit, Jesus, and God are in communion with each other about us humans. Our identity as humans saved or not saved, is that we are made in God's image and likeness, and we are made rulers and overcomes. The fact that we struggle is because sin came into the world.

Originally, we were supposed to be in communion with God and rule the earth, glorifying God, being fruitful and multiplying generations of successful legacies. After we become new creations in Christ, surrendering our lives to Him, the plan God had in the beginning is resurrected. Reading about Jesus' time on earth in Matthew, Mark, Luke, John, and Acts, there are many examples of how He represents God, demonstrating love and supernatural power. He commanded and encouraged the disciples to make more disciples of all nations, healing the sick, casting out demons, and sharing the gospel with power and love. So, understand that our identity on earth is being a disciple of Christ. *Therefore, go and make disciples of all nations, baptizing them in the name of the Father and of the Son and of the Holy Spirit, and teaching them to obey everything I have commanded you. And surely, I am with you always, to the very end of the age."* (Matthew 28:19-20 NIV).

What I love about books in the Bible is that some of the scriptures foreshadow, with illustration, other scriptures or events in the scripture. For example, in the book of Exodus, when Moses had defeated the snake with his staff, and it hung on the rod, that act foreshadowed Jesus's death on a tree. Another foreshadowing of Jesus is in Genesis when God told the serpent (also known as Satan) that there will be one who crushes is head. In Acts, the disciples go out and do what Jesus did before he went to heaven after beating death and the grave. The disciples then walked in their identity, and because of it, they experienced the Holy Spirit in a mighty way.

Paul is one of my favorite writers in the Bible. His testimony is powerful, and his love for God and righteousness is something I pray to grow in. He understands identity and that Christians can never have enough of God and his presence. Most importantly, we are His offspring, and this scripture compliments the concept of being made in God's image. I believe Paul was referencing believers as offspring so that we access our deeper relationship with God. *"For in him we live and move and have our being. As some of your own poets have said, 'We are his offspring'"* (Acts 17:28NIV).

Now that we have discussed identity, let's talk about purpose. Purpose means the reason why something is done or used; the aim or intention of something. Before we were born on earth, God thought about us and what life He desires us to have. His thoughts toward us are always good, but somehow, someway, many people think God is angry at them all the time. *For I know the plans I have for you," declares the Lord, "plans to prosper you and not to harm you, plans to give you hope and a future. (Jeremiah 29:11 NIV).*

Many people seem to forget to do the simplest and most important command in the kingdom of God—love. The story of love is presented throughout all 66 books in the Bible. Paul expresses the vital importance of love and the meaning of true unconditional love that we should practice and develop. *If I speak in the tongues of men and of angels, but have not love, I am a noisy gong or a clanging cymbal. And if I have prophetic powers, and understand all mysteries and all knowledge, and if I have all faith, to remove mountains, but have not love, I am nothing. If I give away all I have, and if I deliver up my body to be burned,1 but have not love, I gain nothing. Love is patient and kind; love does not envy or boast; it is not arrogant or rude. It does not insist on its own way; it is not irritable or resentful; it does not rejoice at wrongdoing but rejoices with the truth. Love bears all things, believes all things, hopes all things, endures all things. Love never ends. As for prophecies, they will pass away; as for tongues, they will cease; as for knowledge, it will pass away. For we know in part and we prophesy in part, but when the perfect comes, the partial will pass away. When I was a child, I spoke like a child, I thought like a child, I reasoned like a child. When I became a man, I gave up childish ways. For now, we see in a mirror dimly, but then face to face. Now I know in part; then I shall know fully, even as I have been fully known. So now faith, hope, and love abide, these three; but the greatest of these is love (1 Corinthians 13:1-13NIV).*

In Jeremiah 29:11, we can read about God's loving thoughts toward us and that He wants to give us *hope and a future*, so we should not worry about anything. The Word of God also mentions being healthy mentally, physically, and spiritually. *Beloved, I pray that you may prosper in all things and be in health, just as your soul prospers (3 John 1:2NIV).* For some reasons, many Christians and secular people believe Christians should not have an abundance of life. I completely disagree with this "pious and poor" notion. Even scripture encourages believers to care for their bodies, God's temples, inside and outside.

God wants us to reclaim dominion of the earth, glorifying Him, prospering, and representing Jesus correctly. When I wake up every morning, I strive to be like Jesus and share love like 1 Corinthians teaches us by speaking life into others. I also speak words of affirmation to myself. If you are dealing with toxic and stressful people, I encourage you to pray for them and pray for a strategy to love them like Christ would. 1 Corinthians 13:1-13 is such a beautiful scripture. Jeremiah 29:11 and 3 John 1-2 remind me that I just need to check in with God when I complete big things in my life. In the world, people have plans, especially in my generation, such as going to school, graduating, moving out of your parent's home, getting a well-paying job, building a family, growing old gracefully, and dying fulfilled. Life would be so boring if that was the plan. God has so many plans for us that even when we grow old, we are still young in his eyes.

In conclusion, our identity in Christ, when known and nurtured in prayer, study, and love, empowers us to persevere through adversities to victory. Many of the prophets, priests, kings, and disciples were in their old age when they accomplished monumental things for God. Matthew 28:19-20 reminds us that this earth is not our home, and we have plenty of work to do, so God's kingdom is established here. God wants to use his children to accomplish kingdom work in the world. Acts 17:18 is such a simple but powerful scripture. When you go about your life at school, work, and church, remember *whose* you are and *who* you are, don't hang with the wrong crowd that can take you down with them.

Destiny Haupt is a college student who is answering the call to be a twenty-first century story teller for God in the digital film and social media industries. Her passion is to help others identify their Kingdom identity and be inspired to build their dream worlds to glorify God with their talents.

To reach this author for speaking engagements, programs and services email destinyhaupt247@gmail.com.

To learn more about the author and upcoming OSOT itinerary go to osot.life.

Top Five Talents: Positivity, Woo, Futuristic, Responsibility & Arranger.

Chapter 8

Self-discovery reveals destiny in a miraculous deliverance from a death-threatening seize

By Shaw Barkat

"The Lord is my rock, and my fortress, and my deliverer;

my God, my strength, in whom I will trust. - Psalm 18:2a

I learned a great lesson from one of my most trying experiences, and it changed my life. It helped me to find out who I am. Although self-discovery and knowledge of my destiny surfaced in a dangerous situation, thank God, that is not how it happens for everyone. Each person's revelation of him/her self is different. So, if you are in great need to better understand your unique identity and destiny, then the right book in your hands. I consider myself to be a common man, so I am honored and proud to be a part of this anthology, "Destiny: The Other Side of Through."

How I got to *the other side through* is an unforgettable experience.

I was born and raised in Pakistan, a country in South Asia, bordered by the Arabian Sea in the south and by Afghanistan, China, India, and Iran. My upbringing was in a middle-class family with numerous challenges. We experienced financial, family, cultural, discrimination, and belief system challenges. Both of my parents' sides of the family were divided by different religious beliefs—Christianity, Catholicism, and witchcraft. Consequently, I was growing up in an environment where everybody was telling me their perspective of life. I was told by many what they thought my destiny was, which varied. Every time I tried to walk on their suggested paths, I suffered from confusion, depression, and an inferiority complex. Also, I was left with hundreds of questions. Who am I? Why am I even alive? What am I going to do in my life? How am I going to do it? What is the purpose of my life? In fact, nobody ever told me or helped me to search for the answers to these questions that are so important to destiny.

Later, I learned that to find out the answers to those critical purpose and destiny questions, we must go to the Source—our Creator. When we sincerely seek Him, He always gives us peace, direction, and shows us how we can navigate the path to find our destiny. The way He showed me the path to my destiny, I never expected. May you be blessed as I share my testimony for the first time, I was able to understand the value of my life and find my purpose.

My life-changing encounter

At the age of 17, I got trapped in circumstances where I faced death threats. This event happened during outreach evangelism. In those days, I was in high school, and it was about the season of summer vacation. I had an invitation to join a youth campaign which was sent and recommended by a family friend. As I mentioned earlier, I had been led by many people to find my destiny but never could with their directions, until this happened to me. So, for two weeks, I had to go to a campaign in a different state. I was so excited, not because I was a part of the campaign, but I liked traveling and going to new places, even though I had no idea what it entailed.

In the first week of the campaign, we heard so many positive lectures about the good news of life and enjoyed fun and fellowship. However, the second week, we were told to go out in the streets and share the good news of life which we had been taught and hand out some literature. First, I thought this would be fun like the other week, but I had no idea what was coming my way.

When I arrived at the designated area where I was supposed to communicate with people and handout the literature, I noticed people were looking at me like I have entered someone's house without an invitation. Probably, they recognized that some stranger was among them. This place was totally new to me. Even in preparation for this outreach, we were taught about the location and culture, but being there was a completely different experience. Anyway, without thinking anything else, I put my hand in the bag I had and took out some books. I said hello to a few people, shook hands, gave those books to them, and started walking toward different streets.

When I was barely a few blocks away from the location where I gave the books, I turned around and found myself surrounded by a large group of people. They were yelling at me. They were mad and were asking for something that I could not get for them. I was shocked, surprised, confused, and afraid in that situation. Then, suddenly, someone from the crowd came up to the front and started inquiring about me. It seemed like he was their leader. While he was questioning me, I observed that they were planning something. Hearing their words, I thought, "Oh My God!" I realized I was captured by one of the radical groups of people who wanted to hurt or even kill me for distributing literature. They didn't allow any outsiders to share anything outside of their belief system because they considered it blasphemy in their community.

My life was in danger. In the background noises, someone said, "Hang him!" and some said, "Stoned him!" Somehow with their leader's decision, they decided to take me to a different location. Someone made a phone call, and in a few minutes, a jeep-type vehicle showed up. They put me in the jeep, drove through the desert, and brought me a place that looked like a prison. After a few minutes, they decided to throw me in jail cell where there were already a few prisoners. When I saw the faces of gigantic people outside the jail, I got so scared. Also, it seemed like they were drunk. I assure you, regardless of how tough, no teenagers or adults would want to be in a cell with them. They were dangerous criminals.

In a few seconds, my whole life started revolving around me. My parents, my siblings, my friends, almost every face I knew since my childhood, was running through my mind. I said to myself, "This is my last day on this earth, and I won't be able to see them all." For the first time, life was very valuable for me. For the first time, I felt the responsibility for my relationships. I was so afraid to think that my parents would face so much pain if something happened to me.

I cried out to my Creator. I said, "Heavenly God, if you really exist, then save me and get me out of this mess, and I'll be thankful to you for the rest of my life." For the first time in life, I felt and thought, "I AM VERY IMPORTANT." While I was going through this terrible situation, God Almighty heard me, and miraculously He delivered me from their hands. Suddenly, one of the persons in charge of the place ordered them to let me go and dropped me off at the bus station. Yes, without throwing me in jail, they let me go with the warning not to ever come back. Wow, what happened? I was amazed. God spared my life. I was released from those people's hands. I was so filled with thankful emotions and left that place without looking back.

Looking forward with new value

Since that day, I have never been released from this burden that I am on this earth, not just for me but for many others who need me and love me. I truly found the path to my destiny by knowing that I am so important, understanding my worth for me, God, and many others. From that day forward, I never stopped my search for knowing myself. The more I know my worth, the more I will know my values, then the more I will be able to continue my journey toward destiny. Since then, I have been living with this purpose that I am very important to help many others to find their purpose and destiny.

Did you see how that dangerous incident became a life-changing event for me forever? I have never regretted what happened to me nor blamed anyone. In Fact, this incident has given me an opportunity to acknowledge myself and share my testimony. I am not saying that you have to go through what I went through to discover yourself. Just realize and understand that you are very important. During my search for knowing me more, my capacity, and how I should behave in tough situations of life, I was able to find out.

Sometimes God allows certain circumstances to help us discover ourselves, our capacity and abilities, and who He is. Until you try to lift an 80-kilogram weight (176 pounds), you will not know if you can lift it or not. It doesn't matter the first time if you could or couldn't lift the weight. But when your capacity or ability is tested, you can prepare yourself accordingly for the task. Preparation may include lifting lighter weights and gradually increasing them until you are able to lift 80 kilograms. This will take discipline and practice while focusing to finish the task.

When we discover who we are, circumstances and problems become an opportunity to show what we are capable of. Then, nothing can stop us in pursuit of destiny. Actually, such opposition puts us in a position to determine our destiny.

It took me some time to understand that I am designed to reach my purpose until finally I got it: I AM GOD'S PRODUCT. A product should never tell its manufacturer, "I do not want to function the way you built me." Most people may think they came from their parents, but the Bible does not support that thinking. In Jeremiah 1: 5, God says, *"Before I formed you in the womb, I knew you."* So, God knew what parents He was going to send us *through* to enter this world. He formed us with the extraordinary abilities not just to reach our ultimate destiny but also to navigate our paths to destiny.

What do you think destiny is for you? Where are you on your journey to destiny today? Many people assume getting their preferred job, having their own business, dream house, or desired life partner is destiny. All these things, although desirable and important, are not our ultimate destinies. Sooner or later, when faced with storms, tribulations, and oppositions in life's path, we don't feel safe and satisfied with that which we sought to originally attain, even though we have it.

There is something deeper within that links us to true destiny. To get on the right path to destiny, we must be genuine and authentic. Realize that every experience counts on the journey to destiny. Whether we consider an experience good or bad, it offers lessons that help us develop and grow as we learn. Overcoming obstacles is a necessary skill in route to destiny.

How a ship captain controls a small ship in a storm during his journey on the big monster sea, is an example of navigating a path to destiny in this world. It can be life threatening. There is fear and pressure of facing unaffordable damage in the storm. But you know what? It's not that the captain is not aware of everything concerning the situation. He understands the responsibilities and focuses on performing his duties, regardless of the storm or circumstances.

By focusing on his designed designation, he is able to use his skills and abilities as captain to save the ship and the lives on board. That is how he beats the storm and reaches his destiny, steering his ship to shore. Yes, we are built to dominate over bad situations and to perform our call of duty. If we're not aware of our designation, then we won't be able to focus on our duties nor use our skills and abilities, which would cause our ships to easily sink in the storms of life's circumstances.

It is very important to acknowledge your God-given designation. You may think you are an ordinary person, but you have an extraordinary ability to accomplish feats. We fail only when we deny our responsibility and reject our designation. It doesn't affect our lives too much when this world or the people in our environments reject us. Damage starts in our lives when we accept the rejection, become offended, and stopped trying to pursue our purpose. That is how we can get off course in our journey toward destiny and wonder in a wilderness.

God has created us in a unique way. Psalm 139: 14 affirms, *"I will praise You, for I am fearfully and wonderfully made; Marvelous are Your works, and that my soul knows very well."* When you know you are wonderfully made with extraordinary abilities, no one can stop you from reaching your ultimate destiny. There is no one who has reached the ultimate destiny without knowing their worth and discovering their God-given abilities. So, focus on who you are and discovering more of yourself.

In conclusion, I am hoping my testimony and teaching in this chapter will help you to focus on discovering and repositioning yourself for continuing the journey toward your destiny. Never give up. You're built to build! Accept God's favor and blessings for you!

Shaw K. Barkat is an evangelist and Apostle to Pakistan. His is the founder of Nation Builders International with a mission to empower lives with faith, hope, and love to see transformed communities around the world.

To reach this author for speaking engagements, programs and services email him at shawbarkat@nbiministries.org.

To learn more about the author and upcoming OSOT itinerary go to osot.life.

Top Five Talents: Relator, Positivity, Maximizer, Strategic & Woo

Chapter 9

Moving through and to your vision

By Ella Coleman

"Write the vision and make it plain on tablets, that he may run who reads it. For the vision is yet for an appointed time; but at the end it will speak and it will not lie."

-Habakkuk 2:2-3 NKJV

Vision surpasses sight with vivid precision into the future, revealing in advance a magnificent outcome to work toward. But it's up to the visionary to transition that vision from idealism to realism. Vision is a beautiful futuristic view as it relates to your God-given assignment or purpose in life. Vision is full of desire, which is a motivator of action that comes from the heart. It fuels passion and unveils purpose.

Vision is interrelated with purpose and passion which points one to destiny. It is essential to understand that purpose is the foundation on which vision is built. Purpose is the original intent for the existence of someone or something, a clear definition given by the late Dr. Myles Munroe. Purpose is why God gave you birth. Vision is when you see it. Passion is when you *pursue* it. Until you see it (vision), there is no passion to pursue it. This is why a visionary must make clear his/her vision by writing it down and making it plain as stated above in Habakkuk 2:2. God has put the ball in our court when it comes to vision, although He is working in and through us to bring it forth.

Divine vision is a glimpse of reality already in the mind of God to be navigated into the earthly realm by the person in whom He has entrusted it. God's ultimate intention for giving us vision is to bless as many people as possible while moving us toward His vision for us—to have eternal life and be with Him as a family of nations, reigning in righteousness in a new heaven and new earth (Revelation 2:1-3). Our current visions should be in harmony with God's vision for us. This is a kingdom concept that can help generate healthy thoughts about your vision and the visions of others. This kind of thinking requires some spiritual warfare.

Vision is weaponry to shoot down the destructive forces of distraction, division, and confusion that are loose in the world. That is why "Where there is no vision, the people perish" (Proverbs 29:18). They cast off restraints or parameters and go in every direction with no offensive or defensive knowledge for survival. So, in a collective sense, a good leader can provide a great vision for many people that will improve their conditions and preserve them.

Great visionaries of the past and present can be quite inspiring for carrying out our own visions. Most of them had to overcome many adversities. Dr. Martin Luther King, Jr. was infused with a vision of a unified America of equality and justice for all, which moved him to fight for the civil rights of his people and the human rights of all people. Although America has not lived up to Dr. King's vision, it still inspires hope for justice in people throughout the world. Born into slavery, Harriett Tubman, abolitionist and political activist, had a vision of freedom from for herself, family, and others, enabling her to lead hundreds to freedom on the Underground Railroad. The youngest Noel Prize laureate, Malala Yousafzai (22), a Pakistani activist for female education, bravely protested for their equality.

Surely, it is more than a notion to conceive a vision and navigate it to full manifestation. It could happen in a short while; it may take a lifetime, or in some cases the vision is carried out by the visionary's successors after his or her death. I share this only to make you aware of the seriousness of a God-given vision.

Vision is really about provision, not just for the visionary but others who will receive the blessings of its actualization. With so many misplaced priorities and unmet needs before us today, there is a demand on us to work a plan that will bring our God-given visions into reality. Without vision people's lives are wasted or destroyed. Thus, each vision in the scheme of God's plan is vitally important and must not be taken lightly.

With few "vision doctors" identified to help in the deliverance of needed visions, some of us must take on the role of the midwives of the past, who made house calls to insure safe and healthy deliveries of new babies. Most people and the whole earth travail, waiting on the manifestation of those chosen for this task. But will we escape from ourselves long enough to lend a helping hand to those crying loudly and silently around us? Perhaps their cries have been drowned out by our own personal cries for vision fulfillment.

Wherever you are in the process of living your purpose and vision, know that if you have conceived it, you must believe it and take the necessary steps to achieve it. Vision gives you an assignment to impact the world and leave a mark for future generations. Make the few years you have on this earth count. Discover and pursue the vision God has put in your heart.

Preparing to write your personal vision plan

When you make a commitment to move toward your desire, God will direct your steps. Many of us are striving to construct our lives without any serious thought, planning, or strategy. Consequently, most people's lives are unbalance and undependable. The result is, the majority never fulfill their purpose for living and end up unsatisfied and frustrated. Developing a specific plan to fulfill your personal vision is vital to creating a productive and rewarding life.

Discovering, writing, and implementing your personal vision is a learning process about yourself. As you grow closer to God, by submitting and communicating with Him, vision can become much clearer. Vision is progressive and dynamic, so your understanding of the vision will be continually refined, enabling you to better navigate and see it manifest. Thus, when you write your vision, realize that it won't be a finished product. As time transpires, it will probably be necessary to continue refining it as you experience spiritual and personal growth. In fact, your personal vision should be reviewed on a regular basis. At least annually, set aside a significant amount of time to pray and reevaluate where you are in relation to your vision. You will likely modify certain parts of your plan as God enhances your wisdom of His purpose for you. It will be exciting when you see your vision evolve. Remember, God will have nothing to direct you in if you never write out a blueprint. So, pause the construction of your life until you *write your plan (vision) and make it clear.*

The following nine steps will aid you in discovering and developing your personal vision plan.

Step 1: Get rid of distractions to focus

Steal way from all distractions and responsibilities, cut off your cell phone, or at least, turn of your ringer and distance yourself from it. Sit down by yourself and take some uninterrupted time to think. Do this as often as needed while you're developing your plan.

Step 2: Search and find your true self

Getting a clear understanding of yourself requires prayer and serious personal searching. There are inquiries you can make to go get defining information about you, which is a prerequisite for knowing your purpose and vision.

Ask yourself these five basic self-discovery questions to draw out and express what is within you.

- Who am I? (Identity)

- Where am I from? (Origin)

- Why am I here? (Purpose)

- How do I do what I am here to do? (Vision)

- Where am I going? (Destiny)

Step 3: Discover your true vision

You will be amazed at how God will begin to open your mind to His purpose and vision for you when you answer the next list of questions. As you begin to see things you have never seen before, write them down on paper, read them over, think about them, pray about them, and begin to formulate ideas of what you want out of life.

Ask yourself the following.

- What do I want to do with my life?

- What am I inspired to do?

- What would I want to do more than anything else, even if I was never paid for it?

Now, open your mind and dismantle any limitations of time and money you have put on your vision. Please, intentionally disregard the opinions others have of you and allow some time to discover what *you* really want your life to be. Dig deep down within to find your true desires and persevere through this process.

Here are some more questions to answer.

- What kind of son, daughter, husband, wife, aunt, uncle, or cousin do I want to be remembered as?

- What type of impact would I like to leave on my community?

- How would I like the world to be different because I was here?

Step 4: Examine and discover your true motivation

Since a vision from God is never selfish, it will always help and uplift others in some way. It is designed to make the lives of people better and to improve society. It inspires others because of all the good it provides.

- Ask yourself the following:

- How does my vision help others?

- What is the motive for my vision?

- Why do I want to do what I am doing?

- Can I keep my integrity while accomplishing this vision?

Step 5: Identify your principles

Remember, as you plan and work toward your vision, stand steadfastly on tried and true principles of integrity. These principles can be found in the Bible and other good books of instruction and in role models. The Ten Commandments are great principles to start with before developing your own. When tempted, refer them: "I will not steal, lie, or bare false witness. I won't worship any god but God the Father. I will not commit adultery. I will not covet."

Committed people, money, buildings, programs and other resources contribute greatly to the success of a vision but cannot replace virtues like honesty and just simply treating people with respect and kindness. Your principles are your philosophy of life. You must clarify what you will and won't do with no compromise. Your principles are your guidelines and parameters for living, conducting business, interacting with people, and relating to life.

Step 6: Determine your goals and objectives

Goals are required to fulfill your vision. List the practical things do you need to do to realize your dream. Goals are distinct signs that will get you where you need to go.

- Create sensible yet challenging goals.

- Write your short and long-term goals in detail with timelines for achieving them.

- After you have written your goals, add your objectives, which are the detailed steps of your goals. Clearly explain exactly what you need to do and when you need to do it, so you arrive where you want to go. Objectives should include specific timetables.

Step 7: Identify your resources

You now need to identify all the resources you will need to accomplish your vision. List needed human and material resources. What help do you need from others to fulfill your vision? Consider personal associations you may need to have and not have? What material or monetary resources do you need to fulfill your vision? Write them down regardless of how large they may seem.

Assess your strengths. Determine what you are good at. Write down your answers, and then make plans to enhance your strengths. For example, if your vision requires that you work with youth, start doing it, even as a volunteer. Your vision may require you to speak before large groups of people, so press through your fear and begin speaking every chance you get. Ask and God will give you opportunities to speak, so you can develop your gift

Write down your weaknesses. Your vision needs some things you are not good at? Don't shy away from your weaknesses because everyone has them. You need to identify them, so God will supply other people to do what you cannot. Your vision will not be fulfilled alone but with people who are strong in areas where you are weak.

Step 8: Write your statements

After you have gone through all of the above steps, which may take some time, you should be able write out three important statements for your life: **a purpose statement**, a **mission statement**, and a **vision statement**. They are distinguished and described below. Take your time to learn the basic components of each one.

A **Purpose Statement** includes who you are, how you are endowed (gifts, calling, abilities, talents, anointings) which is linked to your reason for being and how you will present yourself as a gift to serve the Lord and help his people on this earth.

A **Mission Statement** includes a specific and outwardly focused task or mission that demonstrates the *living out* of your specific purpose and vision. Mission accommodates purpose. It can change but purpose remains constant, so it has timelines. It spells out what you will do in a specific location, targeting specific people. Therefore, it should be compatible with your goals.

A personal **Vision Statement** is your dream or projection into the future of your life. It needs to be succinct, clear, and understandable while painting a picture of *where* you are headed and why. It is big, futuristic, and descriptive. It is the *north star* for your life, guiding you to your place of great impact, causing improvement of yourself, family, community, and world. It should feed the imagination and inspire the hearts of people who read it. But here's why it may take time to craft: you must summarize the vision for your life into just one powerful sentence.

Step 9: Commit to your vision

You must be committed to your vision if you want to fulfill it. Be resolute. You must make a specific decision to follow through on carrying out your vision, acknowledging that God may refine or even change your plans as He leads you through the process. Also, commit your vision to God regularly. So, your commitment is two-fold. 1. Commit to your vision and 2. Commit your vision to God.

Now that you have tools and practical directions for carrying out the vision for your life, you are equipped to get on the path to realizing your dreams. Press forward with discipline and diligence. No God-given vision is too great to realize. Although many human aspirations seem lofty and too impractical to manifest, the truth is, you can attain what you envision, especially if it is divinely bestowed. So be encouraged to move forward with a clear vision and comprehensive plan for your life.

"Commit to the Lord whatever you do, and your plans will succeed." -Proverbs 16:3

Ella Coleman is a speaker, author, vision consultant, president of Ellavation Publishing, LLC, publisher of PURPOSE Magazine, and founder of Purpose For Life Foundation.

To reach this author for speaking engagements, programs and services email her at ella@ellacoleman.net.

To learn more about the author and upcoming OSOT itinerary go to osot.life..

Top Five Talents: Input, Ideation, Adaptability, Strategic & Relator

Chapter 10

The ninja warrior strategy
for breaking through to your fulfillment

By Shelley Fisher

"… we are more than conquers through Him who loved us." –
Romans 8:37 NKJV

Navigating your way to the other side of through is a challenging task. I liken it to successfully conquering difficult obstacle courses much like those encountered by the ninja warrior contestants on the popular television series. Before beginning the course, each contestant stands before a crowd with a look of determination on their faces while the announcer unfolds his or her personal story. Their stories vary. Some were raised in the lap of luxury, some lived the depths of poverty, and some have even overcome physical disabilities. Some are married while others are single; both males and females. You see, anyone can enter the course, but there is one thing they all must possess and that is a commitment to go through to the other side.

Back to the scenario ... The lone contestant stands facing the looming obstacle course with the crowd looking on. A close-up of the crowd shows the people closest to the contestant. They are cheering and holding up signs like, "You Can Do This" and "We're With You!" As the camera pans outward, the faces of the crowd seem to change. They are not cheering. Only looks of curiosity, disbelief, and doubt can be seen in the larger audience.

What is the backstory of this contestant? How did he or she qualify to reach this point? They first discovered their natural ability. I submit that each contestant had to have an interest and talent in physical fitness. They made a decision to be dedicated to developing that talent through rigorous, focused training and research. They placed themselves in environments that fed their talent and surrounded themselves with those who encouraged them in their quest.

As we travel on our journey to the other side of through, we can consider the ninja warriors. We may not have a physical course to face, but it's a course just the same. We must stretch to reach the swinging bars of indecision to keep them from swaying, while maintaining our balance as we jump onto the floating steps. Then, muster enough strength to climb up and over the vertical walls of doubt, gain enough momentum to dash across the slanted steps of opportunity, use the swinging rope to propel ourselves over the deep water of intimidation to the next level. Finally, we must avoid the swinging punching bags of fear, designed to knock us down, and navigate across the spinning platforms of distraction to victory.

Identifying your gift or natural talent

The first step in becoming a ninja warrior is to identify your natural talent. Often, it's called a gift or calling. It is something you naturally excel at doing. It resides in your heart and motivates you. Your gift or talent determines how you select your course. The course you travel shouldn't be determined by what someone else forces you to do, nor chosen because "that's what everyone else is doing." Neither should it be a course you chart simply because of the monetary rewards. Motivation by money alone can be a great distraction. I know people who have followed a course based not on their gift but on financial gain and found themselves unfulfilled. Select your course based on that inner desire which calls out to you and motivates you to push forward.

Identifying your natural talent can be quite confusing and elusive. Here's a hint. What is it that you could do all day and not get tired? Even as children, we lean toward our natural gifts. The little girl will line up her dolls and act like she is their teacher or writes stories about made up lands. The little boy will be the one all the kids go to be the mediator or pick up a basketball and be on the court all day. There's something that grabs your interest and keeps you focused. There is a seed that God planted in your heart that pulls at you.

My natural talent and gifts lie in the performing arts. My father used to be a high school drama coach. He would pick me up from nursery school, and I would sometimes accompany him to his rehearsals before going home. My dad would sit me in the dark auditorium while he directed the students in rehearsals on the stage. I should have been afraid of sitting alone in the dark at 4 years old, but I remember sitting absolutely still, eyes wide, mesmerized by what I saw happening on stage. Soon I could recite the actor's lines, even though I could barely read. Funny story ... I was in the audience on the day of a performance, and someone sitting near me got up and went backstage to get my father. They asked him if he could please take me backstage with him because I was enthusiastically saying all of the lines out loud and distracting everyone. No one told me to memorize all the actor's lines. I did it without coaching. It was something that came naturally because of the seed or gift that had been planted.

Being an educator, my father had a large library. In that library were shelves of playscripts. One of my favorite things to do was to sit on the floor with my legs folded and pour over those scripts. I imagined myself directing the actors and running a rehearsal. I envisioned myself directing and imagined the day of the opening performance.

My mother is a nurturer, and she desired to expose me to a plethora of different things. When I enrolled in grade school, she made sure I took piano lessons, learned how to play an instrument, and signed me up for competitive sports. Although I enjoyed them, none held my attention. I wanted to direct plays! I came up with my own solution. I gathered all my friends at recess time one day and tried to convince them to be in my play. The plan was to meet daily in the auditorium at recess time to rehearse. Many of the kids wouldn't think of missing recess, but I had a few takers. I used the scripts from my father's library. We rehearsed for about a month, and then it fizzled. We didn't get a chance to perform, but I had certainly put my heart into it!

When I advanced to the 3rd grade, my mother enrolled me in a class offered at a neighborhood recreation center to take dance classes. The two-hour class offered instruction in ballet, tap, and baton. The instruction was really low level, but I was hooked! Yes, I was the one who was always front and center during our recitals. Again, I didn't strive for it. It came naturally. It held my attention. When I turned ten years old, I attended a summer day camp held on a college campus. Each camper chose their own schedule and changed classes every hour. Excited, I chose typing, drama, swimming, guitar, archery, ballet, badminton, and French, to name a few. Pretty soon, I was cutting classes to stay in the ballet and drama classes! Seeing my strong interest, my parents removed me from the recreation center's dance class and enrolled me in a classical ballet dance class taught by a former prima ballerina. Thanks to my parents, my natural talents were being revealed and recognized at an early age.

Unfortunately, sometimes parents, guardians, or teachers don't recognize and celebrate children's natural talents. They may not encourage children to pursue their natural talents. But that's okay because that natural talent doesn't just go away. It remains as a seed in the heart. Even as an adult, you can still identify it.

You may say, "My talent is too small." No natural gift is insignificant! Who are you to question what God has planted in your heart? It is precious, it is yours, and it has been given to you for a purpose. A purpose bigger than you can conceive. It may look small, but you'll find that it has tentacles that reach far and touch others. You may think you just talk too much. Maybe your purpose is to be a public speaker. People just seem to gravitate to you for advice. Maybe your purpose is to advise organizations. Here's another hint. How do others describe you? Are you known for your wit, your playfulness, your ability to solve problems, your agility, your creativity or your calm demeanor?

Training and development (growth)

You've identified your gift, and here is where the going begins to get tough. You can no longer lean on what comes naturally. It's time to get your hands dirty and "put the pedal to the metal." Training and development are crucial. Your responsibility is to seek out that which "feeds" your natural talents or gifts and gives them strength. Be aware that there are no time limits on this phase. It will continue throughout your course.

This step is a type of incubation. Let's now liken your identified gift to a newborn baby. The baby has come into the world and now needs the proper care to grow. Who are you going to allow to feed it? The baby is trying to walk. Whose hand are you going to hold to pull the baby up on its feet? The baby needs someone to help it know right from wrong. Whose direction are you allowing it to follow? The question is, who are you going to surround your baby with, and in what environment will you allow the baby to be placed? It's your choice. It's your baby.

Keep your eyes open. Stay alert. There are people who can encourage you and impart into you. There are classes that can offer instruction and direction. Libraries are filled with research from others that have the same or similar talent from which you can glean. Be careful to surround yourself with like-minded people and those who will encourage you and applaud your victories, no matter how small.

My dance training journey gained momentum when I joined the classical ballet class. I was one of two African American students. I became a sponge and soon could name and demonstrate all of the positions and movements. During my third year in the class, we staged a production of the classical ballet "Giselle." It was the story of a girl who died of a broken heart. I was given the part of a Willis, who were virgins that died before they married. As a Willi, I was supposed to look dead. The makeup artist applied makeup on the other girls but was dumbfounded when it came to me. I was different. My skin color wasn't like theirs. Soon after, I noticed that my body was developing differently than the others in my class. My bottom was bigger, my feet didn't point like theirs, and my hair didn't smooth back into a bun. I felt set apart. I didn't feel applauded for who I was. It was not their fault, but it was apparent that my time of being fed and encouraged at that level was coming to an end. It was time to stretch out.

I left that ballet company and joined a black theater dance ensemble with an adult and junior company. I was now in an environment with people who looked like me. I was around others who helped me to expand my skills and dance vocabulary. The music was different. Drumming and urban melodies filled the air. I learned how to move differently. The productions addressed subjects I could relate to as a young black teenager. The company brought in master artists from renowned companies to teach classes and tell their stories. They talked about the obstacles they encountered and shared how they climbed the ladder of success. In the summer, we would sometimes rehearse outdoors in the park. It was so earthy and liberating!

I was motivated to learn about the history of African and African American dance. I remember going to the library and reading books about the pioneers of black dance. Pearl Primus, Katherine Dunham, and Alvin Ailey. I needed to know their stories. I attended theatrical performances mounted by other companies and participated in arts festivals. Now I found myself in an environment that further fed and expanded my natural gift. I was around like-minded people who had traveled the route I was embarking upon.

While it is a great advantage to be people with more experience and expertise, it can sometimes be intimidating. It's easy to become discouraged in this phase. What people say about you can cause you to devalue your gift. You've heard the saying that one man's trash is another man's treasure. Your treasure may *look like*, especially in this stage, trash to someone else. Don't put too much stock in others' opinions. Be driven by what is in your heart. Continue to reach for opportunities to grow and develop.

You may not find the right environment right away. There is nothing wrong with trying different arenas until you find the one that fits you. Community centers are an excellent place to explore. They offer classes in numerous genres for a low cost. Also, community colleges hold classes in their continuing education departments that won't hurt your pocket.

Community groups are most likely volunteers but are great steppingstones. If you have an administrative or organizing gift, some of the groups you might want to think about joining are the neighborhood advisories or associations, civic associations, neighborhood councils, or homeowners' groups. If you have identified that you want to write, investigate joining a book club or writing group. Some groups to consider include public speaking, business incubator, theater, neighbor helping neighbor, communities, and professionals online, plus many others. The library and internet are sources for growth as well. Make time to read about the lives of people who have pursued and reached success in your identified gift.

To put it in a nutshell, remember: don't let others' opinions hinder you, find a group of like-minded people, put yourself in a nurturing environment, do your research, and be dedicated to growing and developing your gift. If your growth is being stunted or you have outgrown the environment, it's time to take what you learned, move on, and keep seeking. Invest in your baby!

Shelley Fisher is a choreographer, performer and play write. With over 30 years of artistic work experience including dancing with the Alvin Ailey Dance Theater. She teaches dance classes, performs, and manages events.

To reach this author for speaking engagements, programs and services email dancingat60@gmail.com.

To learn more about the author and upcoming OSOT itinerary go to osot.life.

Chapter 11

Royal habits for fulfilling God-Given purpose and destiny

By Dr. Daniel Haupt

"I press toward the goal for the prize of the upward call of God in Christ Jesus."

-Philippians 3:19 NKJV

In life, there are what we call *habits*, and then, there are *royal habits*. What is the difference between these? Habits are settled or regular tendencies or practices formed by repetitious actions that are difficult to give up. *Royal habits* are practices of discipline based on God's standards for His royal kingdom, according to His government's constitution, the Holy Bible. Citizens of His kingdom, who are led by His Spirit and practice those high standard principles and laws become exactly what He destined for them. Here, habits are mentioned quite a lot because the royal lifestyle lived by kingdom citizens in this world is so contrary to the wicked system in which they reside. Therefore, many distractions, challenges, and temptations seek to sway them from *royal habits* that empower them to exercise their kingdom authority over the evil forces of the world.

What keeps us strong and together during all these challenges is our practice of good, *royal habits*. Habits are things that we do repeatedly without even needing much effort to do them. They come from the collective thoughts that we build up within while growing in our homes and culture. These unhealthy habits built from your heart, end up defining you and your final destiny. Proverbs 27: 3a (KJV), says, "For as he thinketh in his heart, so is he."

Thoughts and daily practices have an everlasting impact on our lives, so we should be intentional about shaping them into meaningful *royal habits* that lead to our God-given destiny. A habit is like a built-in GPS programed to direct one to a destiny, according the repeated input of good or bad thoughts and actions. Once negative or sinful habits form, they can only direct you to an undesirable place where you don't want to go. Thus, it derails your journey. But the input of good and royal habits into the GPS, takes you exactly where you are intended to be by God. More so, when you form *royal habits*, you arrive at a blessed and enjoyable destination where you can stay forever at your crowning place.

Habits have power to weigh you down and shape how you end up. This is the reason why the Bible, in Hebrews 12:1, urges us to lay aside every weight that easily ensnares us. I like the use of the word ensnares because it points to the existence of a trap. Bad habits are a trap limiting us to place of everlasting sorrow, not God-intended destiny.

Destructive habits can lead you to live a lie of a life in the God's kingdom and thus, trap you to an eternal life of lying before God, which appalls Him. Lying and cheating come through wearing a fake costume, like an actor who imitates a role that really does not depict his or her true behavior. So, choose well, and think about what kinds of habits you consciously build with your life. Build habits that promote and edify the Kingdom of God.

The good thing (or bad) about habits is that they can be passed from generation to generation. The reason God entrusted Abraham, who gave birth to the nation of Israel, with the title of His friend, was that he had showed the ability to keep royal habits. Abraham, through his lineage, gave birth to a culture with royal habits for generations to come. It is, therefore, very important to master the foundational principles of God and practice them in life.

Transferring royal habits generationally

When it comes to your *royal habits*, be intentional, know who you are, and act like it. This reminds me of an old story about an heir to the King Louis of France. After the King had been arrested and dethroned, the people who had done that to him did not want his son to succeed him. So, they subjected him to all kinds of temptations, including women, fancy foods, etc. They said, if they destroy him morally, he would forget who he was, and they will then easily take away the throne from him by undermining his personality. But he did not do anything to defy his principles. So, they asked him why he did not do it, and his response was, "I was born to be a King." He simply knew himself and acted like it.

The king did not stick with *royal habits* by himself, of course, but his parents also played a role in imparting their identity into their child. One more interesting fact that comes out of the story of King Louis' heir, is that, in order to tempt him, they took him to a faraway land. However, his royal habits and moral upbringing followed him there. In other words, when you are full of *royal habits*, they follow you wherever you go. In many countries, some schools have boarding facilities where children begin living away from parents at a very young age. By just observing, it is evident that among the kids, those who come from morally upright families, take the good habits they learned from home and practice them in school, even though their parents are not there.

On the other hand, some children may have come from a good family, but they, being hypocrites, pretend to be good kids while at home, but as soon as they are left in school, they become the worst students ever. Once again, hypocrisy is like a costume that one wears that only reflects a good image outside but is rotten inside. The bad thing about hypocrisy is that, if not corrected, it leads to a sorrowful destiny which strays one away from his/her God-intended destiny in His Kingdom.

The young heir in King Louis' story was probably exposed to bad language, women, unhealthy foods, alcoholic beverages, and perhaps bad music that would make him forget who he was. By just praying and reading the word of God, which are *royal habits*, we realize some things we have grown to believe are meant to help us have fun, are not for the kingdom people.

Today, foul language is more like fashion to some it is linked to the habit of listening to blasphemous, and foul-language music. In as much as the sinful habits bring about some level of euphoria or joy in people, they definitely don't lead to continued happiness and will certainly cause one to miss God-given destiny.

Satan tempts us with the appealing things of this world, pretending to be the father of happiness. Yet, all his promises are traps to capture and corner people into a sorrowful life. However, if you are to be like Jesus, having a great destiny, always putting it ahead of everything, you will know how to use the word of God to define your true self. For instance, in Matthew 4:1-11, Jesus was tempted by Satan, only to use the word of God to stand against him and win.

Rightly knowing your royal kingdom identity, makes it difficult for Satan to lure you from the path of your destiny. Again, this goes back to parents and how they say things to their children. When growing up, some kids are told things like, "You are like your daddy; you are so good, just like your mom," etc. Hearing these statements builds a sense of identity in children. Eventually, when they go to school or face a challenge away from home, they ask themselves, "What would mom or dad do?" Whatever wrong thing someone suggests, they are mostly likely to say no.

This kind of faithful attitude towards life is royal and leads to your God-given destiny. However, it is quite imperative, at this point, to mention that the same good habits and attitudes that parents instill in children, also may be easily replaced by the bad ones. This happens in cases where a child is always told something negative like he is going to be a thief like his dad or will be the most unreasonable person like his mom. Therefore, good habits are built into a child way before they even learn to speak.

The word of God, in Psalm 119:11 (KJV) says, "Your word have I hid in my heart so I may not sin against Thee." Therefore, beware of hiding destructive words in your heart or speaking them into a child by telling him/her how they are the worst person in the whole world. By instilling good words and encouragement into a child, you are making sure they hide sweet things within them, which eventually manifests as good habits.

The things you constantly hear, say, and decide to act on, is the way you conduct yourself every day. You cannot do things occasionally and expect to get to your destiny. Live it every day and it will become a lifestyle.

Speaking of lifestyle, it is important to mention the difference between sin and iniquity. Sin is known world over as sinning, on occasions, against God. But iniquity is a way of wicked thinking, like a scheme or plan, deceitfully hidden, and turns into a perverted lifestyle lived within a household. If a father or mother lives in iniquity, it becomes the duty of other family members, or the other parent, to replace the habits of iniquity imposed on child with the *royal habits* of righteousness. The word of God and positive affirming words should be spoken into the child until they become part of his life. God respects consistency and will surely reward you for consistently telling a child that he or she is destined for greatness.

Daniel was consistent, even when he went to a foreign land. He had *royal habits* in him that prevented him from eating certain foods. The same high standard was with the son of King Louis. God has given us the power to control our thoughts. Paul said in the Philippians 4:13, "I can do all things through Christ who strengthens me." Likewise, accept that you have this powerful promise, so speak it and put in your mind.

Our thoughts produce a series of behaviors that affect us and all the people around us. Therefore, your destiny, however it turns out, will not just affect you, but others around you.

The God's people think has got to be changed. We need to act according to the knowledge God has given us through His word. We see, day in day out, societies that are taught about prosperity. We see them getting rich and having as much money as they can. Yet, in fact, they are living their lives with so many problems. There are a high number of divorce cases in these rich societies. They are always fighting with their children, and we hear of siblings killing each other, too. Understand, there is nothing wrong with having money but when it is prioritized over God and family, it becomes a form of idolatry.

How to make royalty a habit

The greatest treasure one can have for a balanced lifestyle is to possess *royal habits*. Instructions for acquiring *royal habits* are in the word of God. Some of the royal habits we can do regularly include: praying, worshiping, fasting, reading and studying the Bible, spending time with family, forgiving, weekly taking a day of rest, giving, loving others, exercising, eating healthy, listening to holy music, speaking the word over situations, honoring mother and father, doing by faith what God told you to do, being honest and truthful, having clean fun, relaxing, and just being a blessing are. These actions will change our lives and secure our destinies.

The royal habit formula – REPOH

We mentioned before, that habits may come out of a royal Kingdom culture, or destructive earthly inequity bent, depending on how one builds his or her life, and the things (including parents) that one grows around, as they all present sources of inspiration. When you happen to grow around bad inspiration, and lose out on the royal habits, you ought to remember that habits come from our repeated thoughts and actions. Therefore, bad habits can be replaced by royal habits through making sure that all bad inspiration, and thoughts, are replaced by royal ones.

According to Al and Hattie Hollingsworth of BOSS The Movement, a bad habit can only be replaced by a good one. The Hollingsworth teach that:

> "Anything done with repetition becomes easy. When it becomes easy, it becomes a pleasure to perform. When it is a pleasure to perform, it is man's nature to perform it often. When any act is performed often, it becomes a habit. If your will is to be rid of bad habits, then it becomes your will to become a slave to new good habits".

The formula that they teach for this process is called REPOH which stands

R – Repetition

E – Easy

P – Pleasure

O ¬ Often

H – HABIT

The above formula simply outlines how you build a habit. Repeat royal actions consistently. By doing so, they become easy for you to do; remember, we mentioned that habits are the things that you do easily, and without thinking much about them. When it becomes easy, you find pleasure in doing them, and are proud to do so. After the pleasure, we see you doing these often, and that leads to your own habits.

Always follow this formula, think about it, considering the things you do every day, and the people you do things with. Habits can be derailed by the presence of wrong influence in your circles, always take note of these, and avoid anything that does not lead to royal habit formation.

In the kingdom of God everyone is royalty because a King is in them. *"But you are a chosen generation, a royal priesthood, a holy nation, His own special people that you may proclaim the praises of Him who called you out of darkness into his marvelous light"* (1 Peter 2: 9 NKJV). Our Father God, the King of all creation has blessed us now and forever. Also, the Bible speaks of us being little gods, made to be a little lower than angels (Hebrews 2: 5-7). As such, we ought to live likewise, and understand that we start walking towards our destiny right now. There is no reason to wait, one, five or ten years later.

Top Five Talents: Relator, Competition, Futuristic, Individualization & Learner

Chapter 12

Practical application for steady progress:
A story of personal development and success

Do you see someone skilled in their work? They will serve before kings; they will not serve before officials of low rank.

(Proverbs 22:29 NIV)

By Dr. Derrick Haynes

I sat in my corner office and looked out the window at the mountains, as the tension and excitement built. I had exactly twenty minutes before I was to meet with the president of the university where I worked. This provided me with just enough time to recheck my notes and rehearse my points. Whereas, I had been in larger meetings with the president before, this was the first time that I would meet in his office on my own. My role and level of authority as a director made me the perfect person for the job.

As the meeting time drew closer, I took the slow walk from my office to the elevator. As I walked, I felt a peace come over me. I remembered that I was well qualified and ready for the meeting. I pressed the button, the doors opened, and l took the elevator to the top floor where the president's office was located. I confidently walked into the suite and greeted his executive assistant. I took a moment to make some small talk while I let her know that I was there to meet with the president. Making small talk was a technique I used to make connections and gain influence with others. This small tip helped me advance my career. After a few minutes, I was told "the president will see you now" and was led into his office.

Once I entered the president's office, I was in awe of the way it was setup. It was huge and full of pictures, awards, and other items. It was everything that I would have expected a president's office to look like. I had worked at the university for nine years and never been to his office. I told him it was an honor to be in his office. I also told him that I had never been to his office, and he gave me a quick tour. He took a moment to point out a few special items that had been given to him by various national and international figures. I took a moment to soak the experience in. He then invited me to sit at his round meeting table that was in the middle of his office.

Soon after we sat down, another associate vice president entered. He had been called in at the last moment to be a part of our meeting. His role was to use resources from his side of the college to assist with our problem. The president convened the meeting, and we dived into the meat of the issue. After starting the meeting, the president deferred to me and asked me to outline the problem. I jumped in and shared my summary and bullet points, which were typed out. Both men sat quietly, listened, and looked at the paper which I presented to them. We spent the next 35 minutes strategizing ways to address the problem. By the end of the meeting, we identified a way to creatively serve more than 100 students who had great economic needs. The meeting concluded, and I went back to my office.

After stopping for a moment to talk with one of my employees, I arrived at my office. I took some time to reflect on the meeting. I began to thank God because He had answered one of my prayers from childhood. I asked Him to allow me to have influence with others to solve problems. Given my background, I never would have imagined that I would be in a director position, where I would be in a meeting with the president. I was also thankful because, three highly educated men (Caucasian, Latino, and African American) with doctorate degrees, and who held considerable authority, were able to meet to develop a solution for the most at-risk students served by the college. I just thought, "God blessed me to be a part of this group."

Though this is one of many stories, I could tell about how God blessed me. It was a meaningful moment because God reminded me that He answers prayer and will position you to experience success. I will now share how God positioned me to experience this tremendous moment.

For I know the plans I have for you," declares the LORD, "plans to prosper you and not to harm you, plans to give you hope and a future. (Jeremiah 29:11 NIV)

I grew up in a loving family. My father, Edward, was from Oklahoma, and my mother, Willie Mae, was from Kansas. The two met, fell in love, and had a child named Donnie. My father was a successful entrepreneur. He owned both a landscaping and a window washing business. My mother was a homemaker who was an expert at providing a loving home for her children. As I got older, she worked as a paraprofessional, ensuring that elementary students had the resources and support necessary to be successful in school. After Donnie turned 12 years old, I was born.

As a baby, I was able to experience the best of everything. I was a part of a loving family. My parents always provided for my needs. I was allowed full reign to explore the house as I desired. My parents shared many stories about me finding tools and other materials and using them to create new things. Along the way, I developed a love for the taste of mud. This was because I used to pretend, I was a cook and made mud pies. Because my mother was in tune with my needs, she saw my strengths and qualities, and allowed me to be creative and explore the world in ways that fed my interests. This allowed me to feed one of my strengths, which was learning.

Life was good from my perspective. There was never a time that my parents failed to provide for me. I would receive toys on my birthday and Christmas. Plus, I was loved. What else could I ever need? I had no concept of money because of the way we lived. I never realized I was poor until someone told me.

I remember one day when I had to pack up and move from our house. I had to pack up all but a few of my toys and other belongings during the process. Shortly after packing up, we all went to a small place with a door that opened immediately to a view of two beds, a small kitchen, and a bathroom. This was the first time that I had ever seen what I called a mini house. I later found out that these mini houses were called motels. In Denver, during the 1980s, Colfax Avenue was known as the place where the homeless, drug addicts, and prostitutes hung out. And within a day, I found myself among those who were homeless along Colfax.

Living in motels, went on for about a year and a half. I remember one day when my mother took me to play at a place called Delmar Park in Aurora Colorado. As I played, I looked back and saw my mother crying. This was a devastating blow for me because my parents and older brother were like superheroes to me. I remember thinking, how is it possible for me to watch my superhero hurting? I later found out that she was at a breaking point because she was tired of being homeless. It was at this point where I determined in my mind that I never ever wanted to be homeless again.

Later that day, as I tried to come to grips with seeing my mother cry. I remember praying to God because I had no one else to turn to. My prayer wasn't anything great. It was just me sharing a few thoughts with Him. Though I didn't know Him, nor was I saved; I just knew and accepted that there was a heavenly Father who was concerned about me. I asked Him to stop my mother from crying and to help her feel better. I asked Him to help me to never experience homeless again. I told Him that I wanted to be important, so I could help others. I told Him that I wanted to be able to have influence with others. And finally, I asked Him to help me do great things when I got older. After finishing this prayer, I felt a calm and peace that was unexplainable. I would later find that this was the peace of God, which I experienced quite often as I grew in the Lord. This prayer changed the way I lived my life.

Three years later, I went on to high school and found many things that helped me to be successful. For example, I became a member of Army Junior Reserve Officer Training Corps (JROTC). This program helped me to find and live out my purpose. As a cadet, I quickly engaged and was quickly promoted. In my senior year, I oversaw the entire school as the cadet battalion commander. In 11th grade, a counselor noticed my potential and changed my schedule to put me onto the college path. Another teacher took me under his wing and helped me focus on preparing for college. Though I had the support of many, I failed to apply myself academically. This led to me graduating with a 2.2 GPA. As I look back, God was honoring my prayers because He put things in motion that kept me on a path of success.

Given my GPA, I knew that I would have problems paying for college. Due to this, I joined the United States Army Reserve. I was proud to serve as an infantry rifleman. My experience as a citizen soldier helped to give me the focus and determination needed to take on the world. My newfound confidence helped me as I started college a few months later in the spring of 1993. After one semester, I achieved the highest grade point average ever. I was able to maintain a GPA of over 3.0 for the rest of my time in college. Through my time in college, I met a number of people who took an interest in me and helped change my thinking, so I could make it to the next level. Because of this, in

1997, I became the first person in my family to graduate with a baccalaureate degree. Completing college was another aspect of God honoring my prayer as a kid. Again, He ensured that I had everything necessary to graduate. This is a significant blessing because only approximately 33 percent of African Americans go to college and graduate with a baccalaureate degree.

Therefore, if anyone is in Christ, the new creation has come:

The old has gone, the new is here! - 2 Corinthians 5:17 NIV

In the summer of 1999, I found myself talking with the sister of a close friend. After a while, the conversation led to a talk about Jesus and the benefits of salvation. During that conversation, I accepted Jesus as my personal Lord and Savior. Though I didn't feel different, I knew that I was saved. For 25 years, I had never gone to church and never knew God, other than a random prayer here and there. Most of my life was all about what "I did," or "what I could" do or accomplish. I soon learned that God desired to help me live a life of abundance. The next Sunday, I found myself in church. The old me who relied on myself died, and the new me who relies on God was born.

As I quickly grew in the Lord, I learned what His true will for my life was. He helped me to get over my past hurts of being homeless. Also, He helped me to understand that my life was designed to help others while giving him the glory. As God poured into me, I pressed in closer, and He helped me to get more active in church.

And Jabez called on the God of Israel, saying, Oh that thou wouldest bless me indeed, and enlarge my coast, and that thine hand might be with me, and that thou wouldest keep me from evil, that it may not grieve me! And God granted him that which he requested.

(1 Chronicles 4:10)

Fast forwarding a few years to 1999 (which was 19 years ago), I sat in church service and listened to a sermon that increased my faith. My pastor had been preaching about destiny and boldly encouraging the members to trust God for the miraculous. During the service, he taught about the prayer of Jabez. As he ended the message, he encouraged everyone to pray the prayer of Jabez. Full of faith, I jumped up and prayed the prayer and blindly trusted God for the increase. After praying that prayer, I was able to achieve a number of accomplishments. At the young age of 33, I became a director (mid-level leader). This is a young age to be a mid-level leader. In 2010, I joined one percent of African American males who were awarded a Doctor of Philosophy. This is a truly significant accomplishment because only one percent of African American males in the United States have this level of degree. I also became an executive by the age of 41. God had answered my prayers by allowing me to experience great levels of career success while being a dedicated father, husband, community member, and church leader. To God be the glory because he did not have to bless me.

"I want you all to know about the miraculous signs and wonders

the Most High God has performed for me" (Daniel 4:2).

These selected parts of my life story are not about bragging; but more about the things God has done for me. It is about sharing my experience, so others can be encouraged with what God can do for them. In a world where many people are lost and not satisfied with life, it is often hard to understand how a God that you cannot see nor touch, will be able to bless you. According to World Health Organization, depression is the leading cause of disability worldwide, and almost 75 percent of people with mental disorders remain untreated in developing countries; one million take their own lives each year. I believe many of our problems have to do with the lack of hope. We need help, and we need Jesus.

It is so important to realize God desires to guide us through life. Proverbs teaches, *"Trust in the Lord with all your heart and lean not on your own understanding. In all your ways acknowledge Him, and He will make your paths straight"* (Proverbs 3:5-6).

Many times, our answer, blessing, or breakthrough, can be found by acknowledging God and asking for His help. I can't say I've been 100 percent faithful in putting things in God's hands, but when I have, He has moved mountains for me. I am grateful for my education, but all we learn is nothing compared to our all-knowing, all-wise God. The older I get, the more I look to God for his help and guidance. The key is trusting God and allowing Him to guide your path.

As I look back on my life, I have learned that God was interested in me since I was a child. He loved me enough that He heard my prayer and put things into motion to ensure I experienced success in life. My life experience had helped me to understand the following statement from the Apostle Paul:

> *I am not saying this because I am in need, for I have learned to be content whatever the circumstances. I know what it is to be in need, and I know what it is to have plenty. I have learned the secret of being content in any and every situation, whether well fed or hungry, whether living in plenty or in want. I can do all this through him who gives me strength* **(Philippians 4:11).**

As my current pastor always teaches, I have learned to rest in the Lord and be content. I can do this because He is always working things out for my good. As I live out my personal mission to help individuals and organizations build the capacity to achieve their goals, I will continue to experience his blessings.

In conclusion, I challenge you to trust God to fulfill your greatest desires. Plus, I want you to remember that God will answer your prayers if you are willing to believe in Him. The key is to hold on and believe He will answer every prayer.

Dr. Derrick E. Haynes, Ph.D. is the President/CEO of YourCareerDoctor, executive life coach and a present day seven mountain ministry gift.

To reach this author for speaking engagements, programs and services email him at derrickehaynes06@gmail.com.

To learn more about the author and upcoming OSOT itinerary go to osot.life.

Top Five Talents: Individualization, Input, Learner, Significance &
Analytical

Chapter 13

Using your fears for advancement to destiny

By S. Danette Padilla

"And we know that all things work together for good to those
who love God, to those who are called according to His
purpose." – Romans 8:28 NKJV

What if I told you that fear is not necessarily your enemy but can, in fact, be used as your helper? Yes, you can actually use fear for your benefit. Fear can be an indicator that you are headed in the wrong direction, warning you to take caution and change course, or it can even indicate that lack of trust in the Lord. This story comes to you from someone who has lived her entire life afraid— afraid of talking to people, afraid of talking in front of people, afraid of being called on to speak. I was afraid to start a business and afraid of what would happen if I didn't start the business. Fear of relationships and fear of not having any relationships gripped me. I found myself running the other way so fast, yet unable to escape, meeting fear head-on.

I FEARED EVERYTHING, until one day, I came to myself with a startling realization. When reality struck, I knew I would not get any further in life, or even make it to the other side of my destiny, if I didn't find a way to conquer my phobias. And the only way that I would ever defeat them would be by changing my perspective of them.

Once I made a decision to change my outlook, I began to use fears for my benefit. So, the next time I stepped out to speak in front of a large audience, the moment that I began to feel fear rise up within me, I used it as the very mechanism to push out what was on the inside of me. And at that moment, I realized that I no longer had to be intimidated by fear again. My new strategy became a useful tool, helping me to get to the other side of what God wants to accomplish in and through me. It taught me that I have the dominion over fear, and when I deal with a situation in faith, it has to line up with me.

It is time to move with what we have been given and to really walk in what we have been called to be, say, and do. So, fully lay hold of the dominion we have been given to manifest the Kingdom of God on earth that we carry inside of us. *And God said, Let us make man in our image, after our likeness: and let them have dominion over the fish of the sea, and over the fowl of the air, and over the cattle, and over all the earth, and over every creeping thing that crept upon the earth* (Genesis 1:26 KJV).

In this chapter, we are going to look at a few different ways of how to face fear and even use it as the very mechanism to catapult us to the other side of the assignment that we have been given to complete. Once you have journeyed through this chapter, I hope you will have a different perspective of fear; that it will no longer be the giant in front of you but bully you have conquered and placed under your feet.

Fear can be used as a motivating mechanism. If you consider fear as an opposition to what you desire to achieve, congratulations, you are now facing your opportunity. You will never know what is inside of you until you face your own fears. Think of how many people have spent their entire lives without knowing the purpose for which they were truly called and created. This happened mainly because they allowed fear to prevent them from stepping out and fulfilling their greatest achievements. Many have had dreams of opening their own business but allowed the fear of failure to stop them at the door. A recent survey by the social network, Linkagoal, found that fear of failure plagued 31 percent of 1,083 adults. Imagine if they would have surveyed many more? And with the proper perspective, fear could have ultimately been their motivator to take them to the next level of their potential.

As opportunity awaits, the next time you are certain of being called to doing something great, far beyond what you think is even potentially achievable, be aware that fear may begin to rise up within you. It will stir doubt, so you to turn and go in the other direction. I can assure you that once you have viewed fear through the proper lenses, you can then press through and get to the other side. You will certainly discover that opportunity came knocking much louder than the fear that tried to get in your way. Consequently, moving forward, you can continue by making the most of every opportunity with the time that you are given here. *"Making the very most of your time [on earth, recognizing and taking advantage of each opportunity and using it with wisdom and diligence], because the days are [filled with] evil"* (Ephesians 5:16 AMP).

Fear can be used as a bridge to the strengthening of your faith. As Kingdom people, we are continuously going from glory to glory and from faith to faith. When faced with fear, on the other side of it, is a whole new level of your faith. We start with a measure of faith but as we continue to move forward in the things of God, and He begins to call us to step out of the boat like Jesus beckoned Peter in Matthew 14:29, and Peter walked on water until fear came in, causing him to begin sinking until Jesus stretched out His hand and caught him. We always gain when we obey God and step out on faith. Even in our weaker moments, God is there to help us through. Each and every time we exercise our faith, it will continue to grow.

You may even sense the fear of stepping out alone, but I can assure you, the more you step out, step in and go through, you will discover that you were never there by yourself. God was walking with you all along. With each challenge, faith will continue to grow within yourself and in God. This will cause your faith to be strengthened and to go to another level. And the next time you are prompted to step out, there will be less hesitation as you recall how you were able to accomplish the last assignment because God was right there with you, faithful through every step of your journey. *"The LORD Himself goes before you and will be with you; He will never leave you nor forsake you. Do not be afraid; do not be discouraged."* (Deuteronomy 31:8 NIV).

Fear keeps us humble. Have you ever been called to step out and do something and you are afraid to do it? I believe that we have all been in that place before. In the beginning, we are holding on to the Lord with all our might, right? We know that this is something that is unfamiliar territory, and God is asking us to do something that we feel completely incapable of doing, so we hold onto Him to give us direction every step of the way. Then, once you begin to walk in it, have you ever felt ready to take the wheel on your own? The fear that we are talking about here is the kind of fear that will cause us to know that apart from God, we can do nothing, but with God, we can do all things. This will keep us in a posture of humility.

We never want to believe that we've got it from here and move forward without God. This is the fear that we can use for our benefit to ultimately keep us in check from stepping ahead of God and moving along without Him. It keeps us in tune, allowing Him to run the ship and to remain in the driver's seat. *"But Jesus looked at them and said, 'With people [as far as it depends on them] it is impossible, but with God all things are possible'"* (Matthew 19:26 AMP).

Fear is an agent of change. Let's be honest, how many would be open to change? The Kingdom of God is moving forward and advancing at all times. In each season, God wants to do a new thing in and through you, but you will have to face your fears before change can take place. He wants to deliver you from the places that you no longer belong and take you across and into your promised place, but you will have to trust Him to take you across. As the Israelites were moving from the captivity of Pharaoh and the Egyptian people, they had to face their fears and even spoke to Moses saying, "Leave us alone, let us stay here!" But that was not God's plan for them, God's plan was to free them from the place of bondage and slavery. Here's the description of their deliverance in Exodus, the 14th chapter, verses 5-14 (NIV).

5 When the king of Egypt was told that the people had fled, Pharaoh and his officials changed their minds about them and said, "What have we done? We have let the Israelites go and have lost their services!" 6 So he had his chariot made ready and took his army with him. 7 He took six hundred of the best chariots, along with all the other chariots of Egypt, with officers over all of them. 8 The LORD hardened the heart of Pharaoh, King of Egypt, so that he pursued the Israelites, who were marching out boldly. 9 The Egyptians, all Pharaoh's horses and chariots, horsemen and troops pursued the Israelites and overtook them as they camped by the sea.

10 As Pharaoh approached, the Israelites looked up, and there were the Egyptians, marching after them. They were terrified and cried out to the LORD. 11 They said to Moses, "Was it because there were no graves in Egypt that you brought us to the desert to die? What have you done to us by bringing us out of Egypt? 12 Didn't we say to you in Egypt, 'Leave us alone; let us serve the Egyptians'? It would have been better for us to serve the Egyptians than to die in the desert!"

¹³ Moses answered the people, "Do not be afraid. Stand firm and you will see the deliverance the LORD will bring you today. The Egyptians you see today, you will never see again. ¹⁴ The LORD will fight for you; you need only to be still."

I cannot begin to tell you how of many people that I have encountered who preferred to stay where they are at, in a place of bondage, for the very comfort of familiarity. Fear of the unknown causes them to remain where they are, when God has so much more for them. He knows the plans He has for each one of us; plans to give us hope and a future; plans to prosper us into purpose and to use us for His glory. We need not be afraid because He will go before us and prepare the way. He knows the day, time and hour of our deliverance, and He has planned for the moment when He can show up mightily on our behalf. He will fight for you, and you will need only to be still. Just as He has done for the Israelites in the Bible, He will do for you. You may have to face your fears to cross over and get *there*, but God will use all things for your good, causing them to align with His plan for you.

In conclusion, my friend, you never have to look at fear in a negative way again. We may have adversaries, but they should never be able to stop us from doing what God has destined for us to do. So, there is no need not to be afraid of anything. Our God will use everything that we face for our growth. We will always gain something from what we have faced and what we have accomplished. We cannot lose because God has already won, and we get to walk in that victory right along with Him. Fear does not have to be our enemy, but with the proper perspective of it, we can use it for our benefit, never again allowing it as a means to stop you from moving forward. Thus, we can the promised places God prepared for us long ago.

Danette Padilla is a licensed minister, youth mentor, worship leader and leader/coordinator of HeavenBound band.

To reach this author for speaking engagements, programs and services email her at sdp.jesusanswers@gmail.com.

To learn more about the author and upcoming OSOT itinerary go to osot.life.

*Top Five Talents: Restorative, Developer, Includer, Consistency &
Empathy*

Chapter 14

Through rejection to acceptance:

A story of endurance, awakening, and triumph

By Dorothy Daniel

*"The stone which the builders rejected has become the chief
cornerstone." –* Psalm 118:22

If you have ever been rejected, you probably need to read this.
Internalized rejection is a constipating and painful experience that
may require a long process to get through with a healthy mindset
intact. Delicate souls can be nearly destroyed by this enemy of
destiny. Also, rejection can be perceived and responded to in
various ways, depending on the person rejected. Most of us have
experienced it in one way or another. Many are still suffering
from a rejection complex that perpetuates its draining effects.
Thus, if someone you expected to support and care for you,
actually rejected you, there may still be some residue lingering or
clinging to you. For me, it was stifling and will be revealed as I

share my story. But first, let's call out this dirty, clogging force that can block our flow and function.

Understanding Rejection and Your *True North*

So, what is rejection? According to The Biblical Counseling Database, the original meaning "is to throw back" and "rejection occurs when a person or group of people exclude(s) an individual and refuses to acknowledge or accept them." To me, rejection is being held in the bowels of time until it decides to eliminate you like a piece of hardened waste that is unable to be expelled without causing your backside some serious damage. Resisting the urge to excrete due to the anticipation of pain causes the body's natural function to automatically kick in and grant relief, whether it is wanted or not. Be thankful God has designed our bodies so that we voluntarily take action. Otherwise, time will either force us to act or die.

Each time I am reminded of the pain that constipated me, tears of joy escape from my eyes, and I vow not to let rejection, holding onto pain and/or refusing to let things go, happen ever again. Another memory comes, triggering a reaction, and the cycle begins anew. So now, I am committing it to paper. I am sharing this burden and will not be doing the heavy lifting alone. I have family and friends who will pray for and with me. They will help me release the rejection I feel, so that it becomes productive rather than destructive.

Why are we so reluctant to share when all things are supposed to work together for our good? All things include the good, the bad, and the very ugly. However, we are trained either by word or deed to only reveal what is deemed to be good but conceal and hold on to the bad and the ugly. The bad and the ugly are the toxic waste materials that consist mostly of family secrets that are held in the bowels of our soul until they fester, becoming the poison that destroys lives. Abuse, whether physical or mental, is locked away in the soul. Thankfully, we were formed within the Creator, so abuse can merely shape our lives, not destroy it. According to Webster's Dictionary, shape is defined as the external form or appearance characteristic of someone or something; the outline of an area or figure. If we were only left with the outward appearance and were never able to deal with the heart, we would never make it out of rejection to discover the other side, which is our genuine place of purpose and destiny or *true north*.

As I pondered the question of my true north, I was able to relate to the answer on **www.gotquestions.org**. The expression *true north* is based on a fact that navigators and surveyors must deal with every day: a magnetic compass is not a terribly reliable instrument. A magnetic compass points toward the *magnetic* north pole, which is not the same as true north, or the geographic (or geodetic) North Pole. The difference between magnetic north and true north is currently a matter of several hundred miles; it changes due to the fact that the magnetic north pole drifts several miles a year.

My soul is a compass I compare to the magnetic north. It has a tendency to drift in and out of rejection and abandonment, leaving me paralyzed and unable to move toward my *true north*. My Savior is at the helm, and He will never leave me nor forsake me because He formed me for a purpose. He does not expect me to be fully restored before I can help others navigating a path similar to mine. I simply need to have faith that He can and will lead and guide others toward accomplishing their dreams. I can speak about the rejection I experienced because it was the beginning, not the end. I am told that the end of a thing is so much better than the beginning.

Family disfunction incubates rejection

Rejection can become an addiction. Strangely, a person may even look for ways to continue to fuel it because it is a defining portion of their very existence. Negative thoughts such as, "Nobody wants me" or "I cannot do anything right" are commonplace and may even signal that things are "normal" or "good." Rejection may even cause a person to believe a lie such as "I am where I should be; I was born to suffer."

I was fifty years old when I mustered the courage to ask my mother about my father. I had two sons and a grandson, yet I carried resentment for men. I realized that I was not being fair to any of them, including my husband of thirty-two years. It took us twenty-five years to recognize we needed to put in some work if we were going to make it to "until death do us part." We have now been married forty-seven years and continue to be a work in progress.

At some point, I realized the relationship between my parents was merely a sexual one. Sadly, I am not even sure it was a consensual relationship for my mother. I say that because my mother often had a hard time looking at me, and when she did, it felt like a look that said, "You are here only because my life depended on it, not yours." I was evidence of the act and an unpleasant reminder to all involved.

Although I was not always grateful to my mother for bringing me into this world, I can now confidently say that I am. My mother was fifteen when my brother was conceived and sixteen when he was born. She was seventeen when she got pregnant with me, and I was born on November 23, just 18 days after my mother turned 18 on November 6; she was eighteen years older than me.

I was born into a family steeped in rejection. We were rejected as a race, and as women, we were not respected by black men or white people. My grandmother and mother were hard working women who were taught to provide for the men and children because most of our men were raised to be studs. They were bred to produce laborers.

My birth meant my mother had two children with two different fathers out of wedlock. In order to teach her a lesson, my mother's family refused to assist her with my care. I did not get the reception my brother did when he was born. My grandmother and my aunts treated me as though I was invisible. One would think that such type of treatment would make me want to disappear, but I was determined to be heard. I learned to talk at an early age and was hell-bent on not being ignored, no matter how many whippings I received at their hands. While my mother was at work, they gave me minable care, regardless of the fact that my mother's earnings went toward taking care of everyone in the house.

As a way of escape, my aunts either got married or became pregnant in their early teenage years. Yet, their plans went awry. Their pain transitioned from mental abuse to physical abuse at the hands of men who were not taught to be husbands or fathers. I am my mother's second child and her only daughter. Nothing that I have said is out of spite or to disparage my mother and family. I know I was surrounded by phenomenal women, and I can stand because of what they endured. I am being transparent to display the glory of God and exemplify the victory He can give you in your life.

When I was five years old, my mother got married. She had three children at the time and was pregnant with her fourth. The man she married had daughters that were her age, which seemed strange to me. However, my siblings and I wanted and needed a father. We were awakened in the morning by the sounds of screaming and fighting. We fell asleep at night listening to moaning and groaning; I recognized it not as passion or lovemaking but as an attempt to find love in an otherwise hostile environment. We lived in a two-room barrack with no indoor toilet. The property owner called it an apartment. My siblings and I shared one room, and the other room was the kitchen; my mother and her husband used the kitchen as their bedroom, however, there were no doors, and a piece of material separated the two rooms. I would hear them talk and even breathe while they slept, so it always felt as if I was awake.

After several years in that home, my mother birthed three more babies. I am not exactly sure how long we lived there, but it seemed like an eternity. Eventually, my mother's husband, the man who was supposed to be a father to us who were fatherless, left, and never came back. I was told another man was my grandfather, although I only recall seeing him once in my eight years, showed up to move us to a different barrack that had three rooms in a small town in Texas. My mother then had another baby, bringing the total to seven children. She was solely responsible for providing for our entire family. To support our family, she became a house cleaner and caretaker for a white family. It was not until my adult life when I saw the movie, "The Help," that I realized how her life was molded after moving to that town. Sometimes, my mother would be gone for days, even weeks at a time, and I was responsible for getting my brothers and myself off to school. We were always clean because my mother would take our clothes to work, wash them, and somehow get them back to us. I witnessed the hardships she faced as a single mother, so I vowed never to have children until I was married.

We finally moved out of the barracks after waking up one morning and finding a dead man's body two doors down from where we lived. The woman who shot the man was my mother's best friend, and I was told it was done in self-defense. Unfortunately, I did not think fighting was unusual because I had grown accustomed to men and women behaving that way; fighting was modeled to me by my family as well as the families of most of my friends. My outlook on relationships changed that day, and I knew that violence could not be the design for my life.

Calling in the midst of pain

At the age of 40, I began to recognize that I have God's calling on my life. As a result of a terrible car accident, a disc in my neck was crushed, and I was concussed but did not receive treatment until three months after the incident. Being extremely low, both mentally and physically, forced me to look up and grab hold of the one truth I had embraced in life; God was in heaven, so I called out to Him. I spent a year recovering from surgery and learning to deal with pain because I was told pain would be my new way of life. I passed eight years on my backside, which I equate to Paul's experience on the backside of the mountain, in the presence of God's Spirit. While journaling daily those eight years, the path was laid out for my life. Following that path, I went to ministry school, founded a 501c(3) organization called

The Gift of Love Ministry, and traveled back and forth between Louisville, Colorado, and Fort Worth, Texas. For four years, I taught and ministered to families who had one, or both parents incarcerated. We gave spiritually and finically from the donations received through the ministry.

Letting God fill the void of loss and violation

My mother passed away on March 9, 2018, after battling Alzheimer's disease for three years, and I realized that at sixty-five years old, I still had some issues that required attention. Although I shared a little bit of my history, there is much more I did not disclose because it would take more than just a chapter; it would necessitate an entire book. For example, I was molested at the age of five, and it was not easy to keep my virginity after being violated. Thankfully, my older brother, Lee, prevented any other such incidents. Unfortunately, he was murdered at the age of 29, due to his lifestyle. The night Lee was killed, he along with my mother and two of my younger brothers were at my mother's home in Fort Worth, Texas. Four men approached the home in the wee hours of the morning and open fired on it. Only by the grace of God did my mother and younger brothers escape unharmed.

As my mother and I became very close over the years, I recognized that she shared so little of her past because she did not want to hurt me. She came from a generation that was taught to guard family secrets and not celebrate the joys too long because it was almost certain they would not last. The rough years our family endured, trained me to embrace the good times, and appreciate them fully. The good times also allowed me to weather storms while knowing that with God's help as well as the individuals He placed in my life, I would survive. I have learned to be responsible for my own feelings and actions, which has led me to assist others in their struggles. I spent the last eight years teaching at-risk kids to pick up the pieces of their lives, and many have become successful. Several years ago, at Sheridan High School in Denver, Colorado, I was invited to give the graduation speech for the senior class. I am a survivor of sexual, physical, and mental abuse, yet God has used me to encourage another generation.

I do not write out of resentment, but rather contentment, knowing that God is my Father. My quest for a father ended when I realized God was my Father. He has always accepted me as His daughter, and when I accepted Him as my Father, my life became purposeful. My direction is *true north*. I am done being a victim of rejection, and it feels wonderful to have some clarity in my life. I dwell in a place that allows me to deal with my challenges with love, joy, peace, patience, goodness, kindness, faith, gentleness, and temperance. The fruits of the Holy Spirit are not the only attributes God the Father wants us to display. They are also tools to be kept in our arsenal and used to fight the battles we encounter. Although Jesus was despised, rejected, and eventually crucified for the sins of the world, He triumphed over it all when His Father (our Father) raised Him from the dead He chose to glorify Father God. Also, I choose to live for the glory of God and to joyfully declare His majesty every day, and I pray that you will, too.

Dorothy Daniel is the founder of The Gift of Love Ministry who functions as a seven mountain ministry gift, who has a prophetic voice and flows in the mantle of a seer.

To reach this author for speaking engagements, programs and services email her at ddgogem@aol.com.

To learn more about the author and upcoming OSOT itinerary go to osot.life.

Top Five Talents: *Arranger, Responsibility, Woo, Adaptability &*
Relator

Chapter 15

Moving through rejection to destiny

By Dr. Vivian Moore

In my journey, the works of rejection in most of my life began at an early age. I was born in Mount Clemens, Michigan, a premature baby to loving parents who were Christians, determined to live and model Jesus Christ. As I grew older, my parents relocated to Tupelo, Mississippi. My struggle was to be understood and accepted by my peers. The world outside my home was heartbreaking. When I began to confront the stressful and painful knowledge of daily experiences with the guidance of God's word, my real wisdom began. Practicing playing the piano at eight years of age, the Lord began to reveal to me that prayer and worship are weapons to overcome diabolical circumstances.

Growing up in a black Baptist Church, my training began in Sunday School, conferences, and musical events. During those years of developmental and spiritual growth, pastors of the local churches, much like some today, did not believe that women were called by God to spread the Good News. Women are called missionaries, who are *sent* to spread the Gospel and to set the captives free as Jesus and the disciples did in the Bible. So, in my church, women were limited in their call to serve. Still today, in many arenas, the respect, honor, and identity of women are not valued by men nor women who are not aware of their value in Jesus Christ. They experience many struggles to feel free to operate in their gifts for enhancing the Kingdom of God.

I am that woman, who desired a change in every arena concerning the plans, purposes, and pursuit of women fulfilling their destinies. The Lord enhanced my musical gift, and at age twelve I started playing piano and singing for various denominational churches, and special events in local area. I learned that every decision I made would cause a consequence, whether positive or negative, healthy or unhealthy.

The 1968 Civil Rights Act expanded in 1969 on the previous Act, prohibiting discrimination concerning the sale, rental, and financing of housing based on race, religion, and national origin. This Act instituted changes in the Tupelo School system, which was segregated, to say the least. Chosen as one of the twelve black students to attend the all-white Tupelo High School, I was determined to bring positive change in my life that would encourage others to be successful in their dreams. The abuse and disrespect from some of the teachers were hard to bear. Their a task master's mentality biasedly assumed that as a black student, I was rejected and deemed not good enough to attend an all-white school nor fit to learn.

The song I sang in my heart, "I've Decided to Make Jesus My Choice," written by Harrison Johnson, contains powerful words. Verse 1: *Some folks would rather have houses and land. Some folks choose silver and gold. These things they treasure and forget about their souls. I've decided to make Jesus my choice. Chorus: The road is rough, the going gets tough, and the hills are hard to climb. I started out a long time ago, there's no doubt in my mind. I decided to make Jesus my choice.* Verse 2: *These clothes may be ragged that I'm wearing, heavy is the load that I'm bearing, these burdens that I'm carrying; I've decided to make Jesus my choice.* God divinely orchestrated that I be chosen to sing as a lead soloist for Tupelo High School during my senior year in 1972, performing at Mississippi Music Competition in Jackson, Mississippi. I sang the Negro Spiritual, "I've Been Buked, and I've Scorned," which was recorded live. These words still echo in my mind and spirit today. "I've been buked, and I've scorned. I've been talked about as sure as you're born. There is trouble all over this world. I ain't gon lay my ligion down."

My parents spoke these words, "Yes, you can be all that God has called you to be. But it will not come easy." Whenever I would voluntarily humble myself before the precepts of God, then and only then, I began to remove the ungodly dysfunctional character defects in my life to become effective in the Kingdom of God. The next step of training was at Mississippi Industrial College, Holly Springs, Mississippi, in the fall of 1972, before transferring to Tennessee State University in 1973 with a voice scholarship. Naïve to the tactic of a changing environment, the Lord's hand again gave me protection all three years until graduation in May of 1975.

While serving the Lord on an Evangelistic Team and spreading the gospel on the campus, I experienced an encounter with God through a dream. I knew I was chosen by God to carry and spread the gospel. And my pastor during college confirmed the call of God on my life. Yet, life presented decisions, and sometimes my choices were unwise.

The choices concerning marriage rendered some hard lessons. I married my first husband in March of 1975 (now deceased). From that marriage, two children were born. It was an impulsive mistake out of desperation and pride that brought many tears and sorrows. I divorced from my first marriage in 1980 and relocated back to Tupelo, Mississippi. I felt the sting of rejection again. In 1984, four years after my first encounter with marriage, I married again just seven days meeting him. I believed we were equally yoked and compatible. Of course, I had not dealt with my impulsiveness, and emotionally there were heartbroken issues. Yet again, I birth two additional children in this marriage. The second marriage was troubled with many years of unhealthy expectations from me and the chauvinistic mentality he had. This relationship ended in divorce as well after almost 27 years.

In today's society, family ties are fading, and the boundaries between what is godly and ungodly are fading in the minds of people. Dysfunctional behavior has become very earth-shattering. At times in my life, it was hard to make sense of my world. The word of God is a guide on how to respond to the events of life and how to live to fulfill the divine destiny of God's plan. I made a life-changing decision to commit myself to the will of the Lord Jesus Christ. I've learned through trials and the training of life that adversity is unavoidable and necessary, yet life-changing. I learned that no one is immune from suffering and trouble. Through the pain, my personality was developed and formed into the character of God for His plan for me in His Kingdom assignment. Consequently, I was able to make better decisions.

I sought to learn about me and desired the teachings to be Christ-centered. I enrolled in seminary school in Baltimore, Maryland, studying biblical studies and counseling. I pursued to know who I was in Christ. The word has taught me how to trust God, even in the most devastating experiences of life. Through the years of preparation, I aspire to become one of many pioneers in the Kingdom of God as a woman apostle and an entrepreneur in the marketplace. Learning how God used adversity in my life to get my attention is quite interesting.

First, God knew that I was harboring hurt feelings and anger because my life was going differently than what I wanted or expected. I began to feel and see a distance between my husband and me, and intimacy had stopped entirely without any explanation. Out of anger and bitterness, diagnosed with Metastatic Invasive Carcinoma Breast Cancer, stage 3B4, in February of 2006, I began to seek God in prayer. I asked Him what had brought that condition into my life. Jesus spoke clearly and said, "because of years of anger." Immediately, I began to repent with a sorrowful, heavy heart. I had dealt with my thoughts by withholding what I felt on the inside, which led me to operate out of ungodly behavior in thinking. Through this lesson, I learned that I was accountable for my response to rejection and adversity.

Second, the Lord continually reminds me that He loves me and that He would never forsake me. A scripture that comes to mind is Hebrews 12:5-6 (ESV) tells us: *And have you forgotten the exhortation that addresses you as sons? My son, do not regard the discipline of the Lord lightly, nor be weary when reproved by him. For the Lord disciplines the one he loves, and chastises every son whom he receives.*"

Third, I began to examine myself to determine whether I had the right attitude? Or whether I was in God's will and doing what He wanted me to do. I wanted spiritual growth and a proper perspective. I sought deliverance from every feeling of rejection, fear, frustrations, suffering, anger, bitterness, insignificance, criticism, and resentment. This took self-examination and taking responsibility for my own decisions and actions while accepting the life choices of others, no matter how painful. My husband, at the time, didn't want to be married to a pastor or preacher because the call on my life was more than he wanted in our lives. He decided that our marriage could not work. He didn't want to be in the light of a review of his life. I felt and experienced the fear of *fight* or *flight*. My husband asked for a divorce while in the operating room before the cancer surgery. It was a deadly shock right before the procedure. The chemo treatments and recovery combined with the emotional abuse and mistreatment from him was painful enough, in addition to him bragging about mistreating me willfully. I experienced abandonment with much shame and deep hurt. Through my fears and attitudes, Father God reminded me that just as Jesus Christ forgives my sins, I had to forgive my husband. Thank God, I have forgiven my husband, and I am an overcomer by the blood of the Lamb and the words of my testimony.

My priorities started to radically change as I began to set better godly principles and goals. Still recovering from a deadly illness and abandonment, I decided that I would live and not die, to declare the Glory of the Lord all the days of my life. Second Chronicles 7: 13-14 tells me that, *if I would humble myself, pray, seek God's face, and repent, then God will hear from heaven and heal my land.* I decided to *Humble myself under the mighty hand of God, that He may exalt me at the proper time, casting all my anxiety upon Him, because He cares for me* (1 Peter 5: 6-7). In other words, change your attitude and thinking to make and see the results of better choices and decisions. I paraphrased these scriptures to make them personal for meeting my needs in order to let go of the past to fulfill my future divine destiny.

I pray that reading this chapter was a blessing and aids you in fulfilling the divine assignment that God has predestined for you. You may face challenges and struggles, remember God can use every experience for your good.

Dr. Vivian Moore is a Clinical Christian Counseling Therapist and Founder of New Beginning Life Ministries International without walls. Her present day mandate is to be the apostolic of Mississippi God Bless Movement in the state of Mississippi. She is also a diplomat of the National Board of Clinical Christian Therapist.

To reach this author for speaking engagements, programs and services email her at wofaith01@comcast.net.

To learn more about the author and upcoming OSOT itinerary go to osot.life.

Top Five Talents: Learner, Achiever, Harmony, Input & Relator

Chapter 16

Twelve fingers of faith:
Grasping grace to overcome past violations

By Lanora Witherspoon

It all began in the fall, with a pregnant mother of three, baking fresh biscuits. Now, this mother had a special thing happening with the dates of her children. You see, her birthday was on the 16th of October, her first child was born on the 16th of August, and the twins, which followed, were born on the 16th of November. This pregnancy was due in the month of September, which completed the cycle of birthday months, August through November. However, this birth was to be different because the 16th had already passed, and the cycle of 16ths was broken. Prior to the birth of this child, God showed signs that this fourth child would be quite unique.

In a dream, God revealed the unborn child, and after delivery, when the mother and child were united, the first thing the mother said was, "I saw this baby in my dream." It is important that we not only know God, but we must be able to recognize when He is speaking to us. There was another sign: the baby was born with twelve fingers. So, I guess you are wondering what is the big deal about twelve fingers? What does this mean, God? What do you have planned for this child? Children are a gift from God, and it doesn't matter if they are born perfect or not because God has a purpose in everything He does.

There is a significance in the number twelve in the Bible. The number twelve symbolizes God's power and authority as well as His perfect governmental foundation. Also, it signifies all things pertaining to faith and all the primary things of the church. There are a host of other examples of the number twelve in the Bible, but what I have found as the most significant reference to the number twelve is the fact that Jesus unofficially started His ministry at the age of twelve. This is significant to me because that fourth child was me, and my journey to the other side of through began at age twelve. And although that was the beginning, I will provide some background to help you understand the journey.

Soon after I was born, my father left, and my mother had to raise four children alone. She worked two jobs, and my older siblings had the responsibility of caring for me. My eldest brother was nine, and the twins were seven. Of course, there were adult babysitters that helped, but we were raised to care for each other. We went to the neighborhood Baptist Church, and the Associate Pastor and his wife lived in our building, and they had eight children that were around the same age as the ones in my family. Who is better to help care for us? With twelve children around, things are bound to happen (there's that number twelve again). I was too young to have started school, let alone my journey, but I often wondered why I felt very uncomfortable later in life whenever I entered that house. I would never go past the living room. There was a scent that would permeate my spirit when I entered the home.

God revealed to me later in life that I was molested at a very young age in that home. God has a way of protecting us even when we don't know we need protection. My memories were blocked prior to the age of eight, except for one experience. I was visiting with a family that was very close to ours. A cousin of that family, the same age as me, was there, and we were both sort of timid. We were placed in a room and was told to fight in order to be let out of that room. This was very difficult because we would be there for what seemed like hours and then faced being ridiculed afterward. Imagine what impact this has on a young girl's self-worth. At the age of eight, my mother married my stepfather, and I experienced a new beginning.

My mother no longer worked two jobs, she now worked at home, and I had access to her that I never experienced before. We lived in a private home, no longer living in the projects. One would think the worst was over, and I could now live like the other children with a mom and a dad. This world is an evil place because now I was being ostracized (excluded) because I lived in a home in a neighborhood with apartment buildings. My house was the only house on our block. I was told that I felt I was "better" than everyone else when all I wanted was a friend. My siblings were so much older than me, and if the truth be told, my sister considered me a burden. I had a peaceful spirit, even though I never felt as if I belonged. I always felt as if I was too young or too old, and all I wanted was to be around other people my age. My childhood would have been very lonely if I hadn't made friends in school who didn't live in my neighborhood. Just a little more background before getting to my journey. My parents worshipped weekly, and I was sent to Sunday school. Despite the difference in age, my siblings and I loved each other, and we had no sibling fights. My mother allowed me to spend nights at my friend's home, and I had sleepovers at my house. School was great. I loved learning and still do. Really, life was good until the age of twelve, and now the journey begins.

Outside of my bedroom window was the wall of the storefront building across from our yard. In the evening, it was a great projector, and I loved to dance and look at my silhouette. I was totally unaware that anyone in the apartment building across the street could watch me as well. One Sunday morning, on my way to church, there was a car parked with the passenger door open, and the driver with a gun took me to a deserted area under the highway and raped me. I never saw this man before, and all I remember is talking. I talked until he brought me back home. There was another time that same year that I was raped by a different man. Now, my mother had knowledge of this rape and attempted to send me for counseling, but I refused because I felt as if I was to blame. Not understanding how these events would manifest themselves in my life, I soon found out that it destroyed my self-worth, self-dignity, and caused insecurity, anxiety, and depression.

I became what some would call an at-risk teenager. At the age of twelve, I started smoking cigarettes. At fourteen, it was marijuana. My mental state was that I didn't belong anywhere. Either I was too young or too old; too dark or not dark enough; too short or not tall enough. It seemed as if I was a useless, weak human being. This reminded me of why I was placed in that room at age eight to fight my way out. I became a bully towards my sister because she was safe, and I needed to fight my way out. It was a way for me to let off steam when life became too much. All I wanted was to be loved unconditionally.

If I only knew at the time that I had unconditional love from the One who created me, God. I told my mother I was going to have a child but not get married. That was how I was to receive unconditional love. There was an older man, married with children, who took his time to get to know me. Sometimes we would smoke, but most of the time, we just talked and played pool. I was relieved to find someone that was interested in me and not my body. The problem was that I was not educated on predators. This man continued to be my best friend until I turned 18 years old (legal age). By this time, he had me hook, line, and sinker. I no longer knew right from wrong when it came to him. Seven years later, I gave birth to a baby girl. Prior to getting pregnant, I became promiscuous because his wife was questioning if I had a boyfriend and why I spent so much time with her husband. Therefore, I appeared to have boyfriends so she wouldn't harass me. This made matters worse because I was emotionally disconnected from these relationships just as I was 12 years earlier. The difference was that I willingly consented to these encounters. I was extremely unhappy with the person I had become, so now enters my "friend" cocaine. The vicious cycle began, and 16 years later, I decided to leave this situation where I existed to start living.

My journey to *the other side of through* began in 1995, 12 years after my daughter was born. I was working a multiple-level marketing business that was doing okay. When speaking to those whose businesses were successful, the key was the word of God. Once again, a simple thought changed the course of my life. Let me fill you in on some of the gaps of time during my existence. I was a functioning drug user, I'm careful not to say drug abuser because it was not something I *had* to have. I never lost a job or the roof over our heads. It was recreational, and a means to escape a world that didn't love me. Let me add this: during my pregnancy, I did not do any drugs. After my daughter was born, I joined a neighborhood church, so I could have my baby Christened. It was important for me to have God bless my child and to spiritually give her back to Him.

So, let's fast forward. I had not been living my life according to the word, but I made the decision not to play with God anymore. By this time, I was thirty-six years old, which brings me back to the number twelve; life-changing events happen in my life in twelve-year intervals. First, my innocence was taken from me. Second, I was pregnant with a married man's child. Oh, but the third interval brought me back to my first love, God.

Once again, the number twelve represents all things of faith, so what does God have planned for this child with faith and trust in Him? If you noticed in the beginning, I was surrounded by people who knew the Lord, the family that helped care for me when I was young, and God-fearing parents who sent me to Sunday school weekly. We must remember that God is our strength, and bad things happen to show the world that He is still in control. Bad things happen to good people, so that we can show compassion and understanding towards others. God suppressed the early years because He knows what and how much I can handle. God marked me before birth to be faithful. Now, the road to destiny is a straight path on a crooked road. We will make many detours and wrong turns. Even during some intervals, I was an active member of my church. I replaced my negative habits with regularly reading my Bible, studying to gain understanding, and praying daily with gratitude for all Jesus has done for me. Those who belong to Christ Jesus are empowered to crucify the sinful nature and bear the fruit of the Holy Spirit. One last number twelve fact, for the sake of clarity, there are nine fruits of the Holy Spirit. One of the ways grace works is by God choosing us, not us choosing Him. He is not lost and is everywhere all the time. We just need to find our way and commit to align with Him.

Everyone's path is uniquely theirs. For me, it was those simple thoughts, an awakening of my spirit. Those thoughts lead to action, but what prompts the thoughts is already in your heart. You see, after the second 12-year interval, I got baptized, and the Spirit began His work in me. Slowly, I realized I didn't need the world's approval. Jesus died on the cross and took on the weight of my sins. I had to make it personal; He did this for me. The least I could do was show my appreciation and be obedient. By the third 12-year, manifesting through me are: love, joy, peace, patience, kindness, goodness, faithfulness, gentleness, and self-control. Believe it or not, there are twelve fruits of the Holy Spirit. The Vulgate, which is a late fourth century Latin translation of the Bible, used by the Catholic Church, has three additional fruit of the Holy Spirit, being modesty, chastity, and generosity.

Lanora Witherspoon is a Biblical Counselor and Evangelist with a mandate to be a social entrepreneur in the field of holistic community development service which tools to maintain mind, body, and soul with training to handle finances, spiritual counseling and nutrition.

To reach this author for speaking engagements, programs and services email 12fingersoffaithministry@gmail.com.

To learn more about the author and upcoming OSOT itinerary go to osot.life.

Chapter 17

Hearing God's voice: for the other side of through

By Dr. Daniel Haupt & Prophetess Dorothy Daniel

"And whether you turn to the right or to the left, your ears will hear this command behind you: This is the way. Walk in it." -
Isaiah 30:21 (NKJV)

Nothing is more important than hearing God and obeying Him. Following His instructions and directions could be a matter of life or death. It is extremely critical, especially in these last, evil, and noisy days. Yet, so many people, including Christians, are unclear on hearing and discerning God's voice. All humans are susceptible, at some points in their lives, to becoming discouraged, distracted, tired, depressed, and unmotivated. A close relationship with God can be a great help in maintaining balance and staying spiritually uplifted. Life is not made to be cruel or unfair, and humans are not created to walk this planet unguided.

Understand, your life is not yours to live by your own discretion; rather, it is a gift from God to be treasured and expended only according to His leading. He made each of us for a specific purpose and destiny, so He knows the route that leads to our destinies. A person without this divine direction will always be overwhelmed by constant frustration.

Considering the story of Adam and Eve, you will discover that we are all wired to have fellowship with God. We were created to have dominion over the earth. Unfortunately, the fall of man and the loss of Eden severed the connecting cord that binds humanity to divinity. Man was thrown into the wilderness of this world, stripped of his authority and subject to the elemental forces of life. He became a slave in his own kingdom. From the fall of

Adam till now, no one ever gets to the other side of through by being separated from God. There is no dominion without divine communion.

Jesus in John 8:12 (NKJV) says, *"I am the light of the world. Whoever follows Me will never walk in darkness but will have the light of life."* God sees the end from the beginning, and He knows that this terrain called life is full of misleading darkness and confusion. Therefore, it is important to understand, as Dr. Haupt pointed out, that the fulfillment of every in destiny is greatly dependent on divine instructions.

From the beginning of the age, men whose steps were ordered by God are always known for incredible exploits in their generations. There has never been a time when God was uninterested in the affairs of His people. His dealings with the patriarchs and matriarchs of our faith like Noah, Abraham, Sarah, Hagar, Jacob, Joseph, Moses, Deborah, Elijah, David, the Prophets, the Apostles etc., reveal how God wants to be part of our lives and destinies. If these men and women were separated from God in their days, at best, they would have lived an ordinary life, and no songs or stories would ever be written for posterity about their testimonies. If Abraham had not heard God and remained in his father's house, you know he would not have possessed the Promised Land and an everlasting blessing for all generations across the ages. For eighty years of Moses' life, he roamed the earth as an ordinary man, but the moment He connects with the voice of God on Mount Horeb (the Burning Bush), His purpose for living became clear to him, and he was transformed into an extraordinary man. Then, he was feared by lords and kings, obeyed by the natural elements of life, and honored by nations. Because Noah was positioned to hear God, mankind was preserved. God guided and communicated with Jonah, and the entire nation of Nineveh escaped His wrath. How about Hager? She could have died in the desert with her son, but a leading came from heaven that preserved her life and her generations. There is no man or woman in the Bible who attained greatness by being disconnected from God.

Even in our contemporary world, testimonies abound of how people by divine inspiration and direction have been able to break barriers and rewrite history — people like George Washington Carver, Harriet Tubman, John Ray, Charles Spurgeon, etc.

The mystery of the peanut

This is a very inspiring story of George Washington Carver, as told by Richard Foster in his book, *Sanctuary of the Soul: Journey into Meditative Prayer:*

> *George Washington Carver was a great scientist who often prayed and addressed God as "Mr. Creator." One night he walked out into the woods and prayed, "Mr. Creator, why did you make the universe?" He listened, and God said: "Little man, that question is too big for you. Try another." The next night he walked into the woods and prayed, "Mr. Creator, why did you make man?" He listened and God said "Little man, that question is still too big for you. Try another."*

> *The third night he went into the woods and prayed, "Mr. Creator, why did you make the peanut?" This is what he heard: "little man, that question is just your size. You listen and I will teach you." And you know that George Washington Carver invented about three hundred ways to use the peanut.*

God's channels of communication

God has specific ways He communicates with His children across different generations, and we will examine just a few of them here.

Dreams and visions

One of the ways through which God converses with us is through dreams and visions. Not all dreams are direct revelations from

God; but throughout the Bible, God is known to have related with people through dreams and visions. We see how God instructed and directed Abraham (Genesis 28:12), Joseph (Genesis 37:5-7), Jacob (Genesis 46:2), Moses (Exodus 3:1-17), Peter (Acts 10:11), and others., through visions and dreams.

This is what Job 33:14-15 (NKJV) says: *"For God speaks once, yea twice, yet man perceives it not. In a dream, in a vision of the night, when deep sleep falls upon men, in the slumbering upon the bed."* When our ears are too heavy to perceive His voice and our hearts are too crowded to retain His whisperings, God might choose to communicate with His Beloved through dreams and visions. People have been guided and divinely instructed by the revelations of God through dreams and visions. Dr. Haupt, for instance, shared his testimonies of how God revealed his wife to him in a revelation. God confirmed that revelation through the inner witness of the Holy Spirit within his spirit and mind. Today, they are married for 32 years, which is obviously an uncommon testimony in this dispensation. It is established in Acts 2:17 that *"In the last days, God says, 'I will pour out my Spirit on all people. Your sons and daughters will prophesy, your young men will see visions, your old men will dream dreams'"* (NKJV).

Still small voice

Harriet Tubman, the first African American to be featured on U. S, Currency, was born into slavery and raised on a plantation in Maryland. Tubman was in her mid twenties in 1849, when she heard the voice of God urging her to flee northward. She set out hiding during daylight and traveling by night for about 90 miles. By hearing and obeying the voice of God, she was able to rescue about 300 slaves in several expeditions. An account by Dan Graves has it that in one instance, God warned her to turn aside from the path she was on and cross a rushing river immediately. Without knowing the depth, she stepped into the current while the men with her stood and watched. She crossed safely and they followed. Later, they learned that a group of desperate men had been waiting on the path they were travelling and planned to seize them. If she had not heard or obeyed the still small voice of God, they would have been captured."

God speaks through a still small voice to lead us and usher our steps through life. Job 32:8 says, *"There is a spirit in man and the inspiration of the Almighty gives understanding"* (NKJV). His voice might come as whispers in our hearts. He has promised never to leave or forsake us. No matter how deep you have fallen or how far you have strayed, God will not abandon you down here. Isaiah 30:21 says, *"Your ears shall hear a word behind you, saying this is the way, walk in it. Whenever you turn to the right hand or whenever you turn to the left"* (NKJV). Our heavenly Father, through the agency of the Holy Spirit, wants to guide, teach, and counsel us as we go toward the place of our destinies. We hear His guiding voice when we are tempted; His healing voice when we are broken; His encouraging voice when we are discouraged and weak. Even though it might not be so loud at times, it is always audible enough for the heart to perceive and recognizable for His children to receive. However, the voice of God, being still and small, might grow from whispers into silence if we are not properly aligned or positioned to receive His words. So many of us are busy or distracted and have become so insensitive to this still small voice of God.

Through other believers

As you sit in the pew listening to the message being preached, sometimes you feel it so deep inside that God is actually speaking to you. If God can speak to Balaam through a donkey (Numbers 22:28), for sure He can send one of His children to instruct, advise and correct you. God has been known to send His prophets to kings and His servants to nations to convey a message relevant for destiny. Nevertheless, this is still subject to the written word of God.

The word of God

The most authentic way to hear God's voice is through the written word. Prophet Dorothy, a respectable woman, who by the grace of God has an enduring testimony of fellowship and communion with God, shared with us that "God has given us the written word so that we would have a roadmap to Him. The Bible is a roadmap given to point us in the right direction towards Him." Similarly, Dr. Haupt points out that God has wired us for fellowship, and we are His center for communication. The word of God helps us to verify and discern the voice of God correctly. Prophet Dorothy explains that when we perceive that God is speaking to us through dreams, visions, fellow Believer, or through a still small voice; we must check if such leading is in alignment with His character, nature, or purpose. The word of God is therefore *"a lamp to [our] feet and a light to [our] path."* (Psalm 119:105, NKJV). Apostle Paul wrote in 2 Timothy 3:16-17 (NKJV) that: *"all scripture is given by inspiration of God, and it is profitable for doctrine, for reproof, for correction, for instruction in righteousness: that the man of God may be perfect, thoroughly furnished unto all good works."* Similarly, Chuk Colson enlightened that "the word's (the Bible's) power rest upon the fact that it is the reliable, errorless, and infallible word of God." The word of God is tested and trusted. Martin Luther says of Himself thus, "my conscience is captive to the word of God …and to go against it is neither right nor safe." If you feel like God is saying something to you, before you confidently accept or act on it, you must patiently examine it through the light of the word.

How to position yourself to hear from God

Nevertheless, many of us find it challenging to properly position ourselves to hear from God. According to Televangelist, Bible teacher, and author, Andrew Wommack, "One of the greatest benefits of our salvation has to be that of hearing God speak to us personally. There can be no intimate relationship with our heavenly Father without it. But, as easy as it is for us to speak to Him, the average Christian has a hard time hearing His voice. This is not the way the Lord intended it to be." However, through several years of experience and walking with God, we, Prophet Dorothy Daniel and Dr. Daniel Haupt, have been able to suggest working and applicable ways of aligning and positioning ourselves for easy communication with God.

The first way to position oneself for an unhindered life of communication with God is to get acquainted with the word of God. This means you must be born again by accepting Jesus as your Lord and Savior. Dr. Haupt calls this the first principle. He said, *"You need to be created with the word because that is the only instrument that God gives us to task the things we are sensing from the Spirit ... it is very important that all of us develop a systemic reading process of the word of God to keep our spirit man fine-tuned to listening. It is a process of laying the foundation in our lives that helps us to recognize the voice of God."*

Hebrews 4:12 (NKJV) says, *"For the word of God is living and active, sharper than any two-edged sword, piercing to the division of the soul and of spirit, of joints and of marrow, and discerning the thoughts and intentions of the heart."* Pastor and author, Jack Wellman, also observes that "when you examine the Word of God, the Word of God also examines you." Spending so much time away from the word of God dampens or deadens our spiritual hearing capacity and makes us easily distracted or misled in a very noisy and confused world.

The second stage after the foundation has been laid through the word of God is a need to deliberately grow a communicative life with God through prayer. Pastor, author, and magazine editor, A. W. Tozer, says: "if you do all the talking when you pray, how will you ever hear God's answer." In the same vein, Andy Murray opines correctly that "prayer is not monologue, but dialogue; God's voice is its most essential part. Listening to God's voice is the secret, the assurance that He will listen to mine." Prayer is not a ritual or an act of speaking to an invisible God. It is a relationship and fellowship to a conversational Father. Prayer becomes boring, monotonous, and empty when you do all the talking, and God does all the listening. You must deliberately wait at some points and expect to hear God's response.

Prophet Dorothy advises us to always wait and listen before rushing out of the place of prayer. She suggests when we feel God is saying something to us, maybe through His word or His whispers, we must pause and pay attention. In the words of renowned author, Rick Warren, "We often miss hearing God's voice simply because we aren't paying attention." As we pray or study the word of God, we should have our pen and jotter close to capture and document such wonderful moments with God. A popular Chinese proverb says, "The faintest ink is better than the sharpest memory."

Finally, it has been established that getting to the other side of through is largely dependent on hearing God and allowing Him to lead us in the direction of our destinies. Everyone has a destiny and purpose that is a direct route but not a straight line. We can be distracted or discouraged along the way, but when we position ourselves for easy communication with God, He will guide us to a fulfilled and productive life. Amen.

TOP FIVE TALENTS: *Futuristic, Connectedness, Belief, Arranger &*
Learner

Chapter 18

Imagination can take you there

By Dr. Jimmie Reed

... "keep this forever in the imagination of the thoughts of the
heart of thy people, and prepare their heart unto thee"... -2
Chronicles 29:18

My vision for this chapter is that it will offer you a fresh look at how effective your mind can be in helping you to move forward. God gave you the capacity to see images or concepts of what is actually absent to the senses, which is imagination. Imagination is defined as the faculty of imaging, or of forming mental images or concepts of what is not actually present to the senses.

This is a gift and a useful tool when used for God's kingdom purposes and your advancement. During our lives, we encounter obstacles that seemingly make us feel stuck. No matter what is happening in your life; no matter how the trials and tribulations come and overwhelm you, just remember, you are walking out your life on a pathway that is in motion, taking you to another place.

I personally have found that when I'm in a place of question marks about my life and doubt begins to set in, using my imagination gives me hope. I want to encourage you that imagination is a very real tool that has assisted me in my movement forward and can do the same for you. It gives me something to reach for. As I apply my imagination, it begins to develop a goal to reach towards. It causes a stirring in me that I had not experienced previously. The imagery in my mind begins to bring forth positive thoughts that sounds like this in my mind: "wow I think this very thing can become real!" Again, it gives me hope that I can get to the other side of a challenging situation.

There is a purpose for you while traveling your life's road. Imagination helps us push through because everything isn't always what it seems to be. In other words, what you may be going through at any particular time, perhaps even now, does not mean you will be going through it six months or one year from now because you have a special mind-elevating gift. You have been given a brilliant tool that can be used any time you desire—your imagination.

There is someone I know personally who told me when he was a child, what he wanted to be when he grew up. This person is in their fifteenth year of that particular career, which was his childhood desire. Being in that profession was his dream and what he imagined for himself. He once told me, he has never regretted his choice and continues to advance upward.

Have hope. Use your imagination to create options that will extend and broaden the original vision you have for yourself. Imagination can catapult you into something that is completely new! Think big as you pursue what you imagine. You will begin to see yourself, not only drawing nearer to your goal, but envisioning different avenues of expansion that surrounds your dream. So, dream big!

Imagination comes through the unseen or mystical realm and produces that which is seen. We experience products created through someone's imagination every day. After all, someone imagined every style of chair you've ever sat in, every model of car you've ever driven, and the type of house/apartment you have ever lived in.

Do not say words that can sabotage you and hold up what you are called to pursue. You must realize your words carry a frequency that once in the atmosphere, sets itself on a forever journey. The words you speak and the thoughts you think will start a frequency that attaches to the entire universe. Because you have been made with great power, those words will make sure it will reach its destiny as spoken. Use your imagination to produce positive energy that will cause a much better outcome.

Be encouraged that you have a destiny to be pursued. Be assured that no matter what things may look like now, there is always another side. As you keep moving forward, remember that you are significant. God said that He has more for you than you could ever ask or think. That is how significant you are to Him, so allow your imagination to take you to the opposite side of negativity. Let your imagination to take you there, to a place of fulfillment and destiny. Join God in His thoughts for you. He declares, "For I know the thoughts that I think toward you, ... thoughts of peace and not evil, to give you a future and a hope" (Jeremiah 29:1).

Many years ago, I imagined being able to hear clearly from God and speaking to others what I was hearing, seeing people relieved of pain and sickness, and sensing what was happening in the spiritual realm. My imagination was not in vain because many have attested to these same types of experiences. However, I imagine becoming more excellent in every aspect of my targeted pursuit. As long as I imagine this, my pursuit will take me through to the other side.

Some people think imagination is not important. However, in God's word, He said, "Let Us go down... because they will be able to do whatever they have imagined" (Genesis 11:6). They were building a tower called Babel. Also, Jesus said, "Again I say to you, if any two of you agree on earth concerning anything that they ask, it will be done for them for them by my Father in heaven" (Matthew 18:19). A question could be, "Why bother praying, asking or seeking if can't see ahead what you are asking for?" The response to such an inquiry is that believing requires us to walk by faith and not by sight but when we combine faith with imagination, we can see ahead seeing what we believe.

I hope this chapter has encouraged you to allow a new way of thought to ponder and even say to yourself, "I will embark on the imagination journey because it could help get to my destiny on the other side of through."

Dr. Jimmie Reed is an author, speaker, transformational leader, and the founder of Global Manifestations. She is seven mountain leader who functions as a general who activates leadership operatives to fulfil their mandates as eagles.

To reach this author for speaking engagements, programs and services email globalmanifestations@gmail.com.

To learn more about the author and upcoming OSOT itinerary go to osot.life..

TOP FIVE TALENTS: Responsibility, Strategic, Achiever, Maximizer &Relator

Chapter 19

Your ambitious goals can get you
to the other side of through

by Dr. Katrina Ferguson

"I press toward the goal for the prize of the upward call ..." –
Philippians 3:14 NKJV

Goal setting—two words that strike fear in the hearts of even the most accomplished strong people. How often we set out to achieve something and find that somewhere along the way, we get sidetracked, sideswiped, swindled, or for whatever reason, we do not achieve them.

With all that I have accomplished, and sometimes accomplished simply means completed, there is a key that has driven me to completion over incompletion; from an unfinished work to a finished work. That key is simply understanding the purpose and the destiny of the thing that I am writing or involved in creating.

"Always remember, if your why is big enough, the how will take care of itself."

Finally, brothers, whatever is true, whatever is honorable, whatever is just, whatever is pure, whatever is lovely, whatever is commendable, if there is any excellence, if there is anything worthy of praise, thing about these things. Philippians 4:8 ESV

Hot does not even begin to describe the weather on this particular Independence Day. The sweltering heat of July was thick and muggy. The dense humidity felt as if you were walking through a steam room or maybe even the jungle. As heavy as the air was, her heart was heavier. At the time, her children were fifteen, fourteen, and seven years of age. Although she faced one of the most difficult seasons of her life, she had done a good job of hiding her pain. Putting on a positive face was important since her daughters looked to her for strength, guidance, and motherly wisdom.

Independence Day . . . how ironic.

That specific day, the drive home seemed longer than normal, as every stop light seemed perfectly timed to prevent her from reaching their home. Road construction seemed to pop up instantaneously. This holiday was not as joyous as some of the others had been. Not because of the meaning of Independence Day, but because of the direction her life seemed to be going. The sky darkened long before dusk as storm clouds blotted out the sun and put a slight chill in the air. As suddenly as the temperature dropped, so did the rain . . . and her tears. Her oldest daughter noticed but did not dare to ask why her mother wept. She was old enough to pick up on the context clues and realized that life as they knew it was about to change.

Independence Day . . . how ironic.

The closer they got to the family home, the more her heart rate increased. By the time she finally pulled into the long driveway, she was on the verge of hyperventilating. God seemed to be sending down rain with fury as the large, heavy raindrops pounded against the windshield with the same speed and intensity of the tears leaving her eyes. Her thoughts raced like the winds of the storms. There were to be no fireworks on this day, at least none in the skies. The storm made sure of that.

Independence Day . . . how ironic.

The goal was to celebrate fifty years of marriage with him. As she sat there sobbing outside their home, she knew that would not be their reality. There is a saying that time will either promote you or expose you. That not only goes for people; it also goes for relationships. She tried. Really, she did. Irreconcilable differences are . . . well . . . irreconcilable. There were only two real choices. She could continue down this dead-end street, unhappy and unfulfilled, risking her self-confidence while nullifying every lesson she had taught her girls about what a relationship built on love and trust should look like, or she could leave the relationship and hope for a do over.

Despite having Biblical grounds for divorce, she never intended to leave. She had done everything *she* could to make it work. She fasted, prayed, and sought counseling . . . everything. That Fourth of July, she learned a lesson that would follow her for the rest of her life. The lesson was although God answers prayers, He would never go against the will of one man to answer the prayers of another. We all have a right to our own will. Our choice is between God's perfect will for our lives and His permissive will. All we can do is trust that whatever happens, God will use it for our good.

Independence Day . . . how ironic.

You may be asking yourself how I know so much about how she felt in the midst of the challenges she faced. I know because I am the woman. This was one of the most difficult seasons in my life; one I thought I would never get through. What I found though, was that this was one of my most tremendous times of growth. We have all heard it, said that "if it does not kill you, it makes you stronger." This was a strength-building season in my life. The days, weeks, months, and years to follow would present many other challenges that would strengthen me as well. I'm reminding myself that these seasons are just moments of time, in time. Keeping in mind that these seasons do not last forever, just as winter eventually turns to spring, allowing us to go through them more gracefully. Just remember, the seasons come to pass. That is their design. There is a beginning and praise the Lord, there is an end.

Through all the challenging seasons of my life, I discovered a foundational truth that serves as fertilizer to help you grow through *every* difficult situation. This wisdom separates kings from paupers, the successful from the unsuccessful. This wisdom can cause anyone to achieve the success they desire. That piece of wisdom is simply your *WHY,* getting an understanding of *WHY* you were created. A clearly defined *WHY* will help you know your God-breathed purpose. God had something specific in mind for every one of us before the beginning of time, a definitive problem for us to solve. Our journey through this life is to discover His purpose and plan for our lives and ultimately live it. Being clear about that purpose or *WHY* will serve as an anchor in the turbulent waters of our journey.

Knowing *WHY* you were created is more important than knowing your name. Your reasons for doing something come first. The answers come later. If you are clear about your *WHY*, then the path to success is easier to find and follow, even when it gets rough. Your *WHY* is to your life what fuel is to a rocket. It blasts you into the future, in the direction that *you* need to move in to obtain absolute fulfillment and success. The key freedoms that we crave, freedom to do what we choose with our time and money will only become evident as we get crystal clear about *WHY* we were created in the first place.

Being clear on my *WHY* meant that as the challenges continued to come forward, I focused on finding a way through them without losing sight of who I was created to be. I have built all the success in my life around this principle and have taught others all around the world to do the same. What that means is this: if your "WHY" is big enough, if your "WHY" is strong enough, if your "WHY" is huge enough, then *how* to do that thing will take care of itself.

Unfortunately (or fortunately, depending on how you look at it), knowing your *WHY* does not mean that your journey to success will always be easy, just that it will be worth it. It means that what you are going through, you can actually grow through, so that ultimately, your greatness will show through. It is totally up to you. When you realize that your decision to pursue your *WHY* is greater than any of the circumstances of your life, you will take everything that happens in stride, simply as part of the process of your growth and development, and will work together with all the other circumstances of your life to bring you to your goal. Without a BIG WHY, small obstacles are seemingly insurmountable. With a big *WHY*, the large obstacles become *absolutely invisible*. What this means is "if your *WHY* is *big* enough, the *hows* will take care of themselves."

For me, my *WHY* was my kids. I have added to my *WHY*, but my family has always been the foundation that made me get out of bed and push toward my goals, even when I did not feel like doing so. As I grew through what I was going through (a success tip), I began to look at how and WHY I was created and what it was that God wanted from my life. I studied the Bible to determine who I was in Christ, since the creator of a thing is the best resource for information about how the thing works or should work. Dr. Myles Munroe says, "if you don't know the use of a thing, abuse is inevitable." In the process of finding my purpose, there were several "WHY" Wisdom Keys that helped me along the journey. Due to space restrictions, I will only share five of them here. Email me at the address below to receive access to the manuscript that includes five full "WHY" Wisdom Keys and information about how to receive the rest!!

Prayerfully, you will be blessed by what is shared here:

"WHY" Wisdom Key No. 1: *Successful people have a BIG WHY that causes them to do what is necessary, even when they do not feel like it.*

"But watch yourselves lest your hearts be weighed down with dissipation and drunkenness and cares of this life, and that day come upon you suddenly like a trap. For it will come upon all who dwell on the face of the whole earth. But stay awake at all times, praying that you may have strength to escape all these things that are going to take place, and to stand before the Son of Man." Luke 21:34-36 ESV

"WHY" Wisdom Key No. 2: *Successful people use adversity as fuel to propel them to their goals.*

"Not that I have already obtained this or am already perfect, but I press on to make it my own, because Christ Jesus has made me his own." Philippians 3:12 ESV

"WHY" Wisdom Key No. 3: *Successful people do what they must do now so that ultimately, they can have and do what they desire.*

"If anyone would come after me, let him deny himself and take up his cross daily and follow me." Luke 9:23 ESV

"WHY" Wisdom Key No. 4: *Successful people never ever give up on their dreams, yet they do separate themselves from negative thinking, people, and habits.*

"Now faith is the assurance of things hoped for, the conviction of things not seen." Hebrews 11:1 ESV

"In the same way, let your light shine before others, so that they may see your good works and give glory to your Father who is in heaven." Matthew 5:16 ESV

"WHY" Wisdom Key No. 5: *Successful people distract themselves from their distractions.*

"So let's keep focused on that goal, those of us who want everything God has for us. If any of you have something else in mind, something less than total commitment, God will clear your blurred vision - you'll see it yet!" Hebrews 12:15 ESV

It is very difficult for me to give you everything you need in life to be prosperous in this short chapter. Success comes from a combination of thoughts and actions. What I do know for sure is that knowing your *WHY*—your reason for being—is one of the most important variables for your success. There must be a strong enough reason *WHY* you want to succeed. There must be something that gives you the necessary energy to keep going when all the odds are against you. We all have one thing in common: a *BIG WHY* will move you in the directions that will bring fulfillment into your life and the lives of others that you touch through your actions. Whatever you do, find your *WHY* and fly. Live a life so powerful that people will want to read your story and point to you as an example of greatness!

EXERCISE

Have you figured out your *WHY*? If you were already clear on your *WHY*, maybe it's time to renew it. Write yourself a letter. Start it by saying how much you love yourself; we do not tell ourselves that enough. Then, begin to write your *WHY*. Why do you need to be successful? Who are the people in your life for which you have to become the best version of "you" to support? Is there something in your heart that keeps you awake at night dreaming of the possibilities for your life? Is there a cause that you can get behind and work toward to make the world a better place? Everyone reading this may have a different answer, yet we will all have a *WHY*. Once you have written the letter, put it somewhere visibly convenient, so you can see it often. It will serve as a reminder and inspiration for you to stay the course of living on purpose and doing destiny.

Dr. Katrina Ferguson is a motivational speaker, author and entrepreneur. In her unique, uncompromising style, she brings

life changing principles and leadership skills to inspire and motivate thousands across age, gender and industry lines.

To reach this author for speaking engagements, programs and services email Katrina@KatrinaFerguson.com.

To learn more about the author and upcoming OSOT itinerary go to osot.life.

PROJECT TEN

IN THE RIGHT HANDS, THIS BOOK WILL CHANGE LIVES AND CHANGE THE WORLD!

Ninety-seven percent of people who need this message will not be looking for this book. Only three percent of all people understand that they have a purpose and destiny to fulfill.

To change the lives of the ninety-seven percent, you need to put a copy of this book in their hands. so this message that God has a purpose and destiny that is a direct route, but not a straight line will give them hope, vision and purpose

"What do you make of this? A farmer planted seed. As he scattered the seed, some of it fell on the road, and birds ate it. Some fell in the gravel; it sprouted quickly but didn't put down roots, so when the sun came up it withered just as quickly. Some fell in the weeds; as it came up, it was strangled by the weeds. Some fell on good earth, and produced a harvest beyond his wildest dreams." Matthew 13:3-8 (MSG)

Our ministry is constantly seeking synergy partners to find the good ground; the people who need this anointed message the most to become the three percenters who intentionally act on their purpose to fulfill their destiny.

> ACTIVATE YOUR DESTINY THOUGHT
> MINISTRY BY SOWING
> 3 BOOKS, 5 BOOKS, 10 BOOK OR MORE TODAY
> AND BECOME A DESTINY THOUGHT LEADER

Let us know how you are transforming lives at project10@voiceofdestiny.org. Tell us how you are advancing the movement of Project Ten by turning the 97% to the 3% who are fulfilling purpose.

Discover your top five talents and act on your dreams

The 34 Strengths

Achiever

People especially talented in the Achiever theme have a great deal of stamina and work hard.

Activator

People especially talented in the Activator theme can make things happen by turning thoughts into action.

Adaptability

People especially talented in the Adaptability theme prefer to "go with the flow."

Analytical

People especially talented in the Analytical theme search for reasons and causes.

Arranger

People especially talented in the Arranger theme can organize, but they also have a flexibility that complements this ability.

Belief

People especially talented in the Belief theme have certain core values that are unchanging

Command

People especially talented in the Command theme have presence

Communication

People especially talented in the Communication theme generally find it easy to put their thoughts into words.

Competition

People especially talented in the Competition theme measure their progress against the performance of others.

Connectedness

People especially talented in the Connectedness theme have faith in the links between all things.

Consistency

People especially talented in the Consistency theme are keenly aware of the need to treat people the same.

Context

People especially talented in the Context theme enjoy thinking about the past.

Deliberative

People especially talented in the Deliberative theme are best described by the serious care they take in making decisions or choices.

Developer

People especially talented in the Developer theme recognize and cultivate the potential in others.

Discipline

People especially talented in the Discipline theme enjoy routine and structure

Empathy

People especially talented in the Empathy theme can sense the feelings of other people by imagining themselves in others' lives or others' situations.

Focus

People especially talented in the Focus theme can take a direction, follow through, and make the corrections necessary to stay on track.

Futuristic

People especially talented in the Futuristic theme are inspired by the future and what could be.

Harmony

People especially talented in the Harmony theme look for consensus

Ideation

People especially talented in the Ideation theme are fascinated by ideas.

Includer

People especially talented in the Includer theme are accepting of others.

Individualization

People especially talented in the Individualization theme are intrigued with the unique qualities of each person.

Input

People especially talented in the Input theme have a craving to know more

Intellection

People especially talented in the Intellection theme are characterized by their intellectual activity.

Learner

People especially talented in the Learner theme have a great desire to learn and want to continuously improve.

Maximizer

People especially talented in the Maximizer theme focus on strengths as a way to stimulate personal and group excellence.

Positivity

People especially talented in the Positivity theme have an enthusiasm that is contagious

Relator

People who are especially talented in the Relator theme enjoy close relationships with others.

Responsibility

People especially talented in the Responsibility theme take psychological ownership of what they say they will do.

Restorative

People especially talented in the Restorative theme are adept at dealing with problems

Self-assurance

People especially talented in the Self-Assurance theme feel confident in their ability to manage their own lives.

Significance

People especially talented in the Significance theme want to be very important in the eyes of others.

Strategic

People especially talented in the Strategic theme create alternative ways to proceed.

Woo

People especially talented in the Woo theme love the challenge of meeting new people and winning them over.

Discover your Top 5 talents and get coached to living your strengths at strengths@OSOT.life

VOICE OF DESTINY MINISTRIES

Dr. Daniel Haupt, MBA. D.Min.

Website: www.voiceofdestiny.org

Email: drhaupt@voiceofdestiny.org

Voice of Destiny Podcast / The OSOT Series

Destiny Life Coaching and Workshops

Danmil Travel

For Information on Travel Services
and opportunities to meet our
OSOT collaborative writers
visit www.danmiltravel.com

To register for upcoming destination events and
retreats or our next Summer Destiny Cruise email
osot@danmiltravel.com

Made in the USA
Lexington, KY
11 December 2019